COLLINS
GEM

FRENCH
VERB
TABLES

Collins
London and Glasgow

Series Editor
Richard H. Thomas

Editor
Lesley A. Robertson

First Published 1980
Reprint 10 9 8 7

ISBN 0 00 459305 7

Printed in Great Britain by
Collins Clear-Type Press

INTRODUCTION

'Le verbe est l'âme d'une langue'. Duhamel's words highlight the central position occupied by the verb in language structure; yet, textbooks frequently reduce to a minimum the amount of space dealing with French verbs and the problems they present. This imbalance, which may result in the user being familiar solely with a few of the most common forms, can only be corrected by studying verbs in depth.

In addition to basic information about verbs and how to use them, this book provides:

★ 112 fully conjugated verb models
★ over 2000 common verbs, each cross-referred to its basic model, in an alphabetically arranged index
★ major constructions and idiomatic phrases for most verb models
★ similarly conjugated verbs with translations for numerous verb types

You are forewarned of some of the pitfalls that you, as an English-speaking user of French verbs, may encounter and are supplied with a glossary of grammatical terms. For fuller details, see below.

CONTENTS

THE FRENCH VERB

The majority of verbs are regular and conform to rules; the fact that irregular verbs do not follow any overall pattern means that they have to be learned individually.

The Infinitive ending of regular verbs indicates to which Conjugation or group they belong:

1st Conjugation: ER ending; model: DONNER (36)*
2nd Conjugation: IR ending; model: FINIR (45)*
3rd Conjugation: RE ending; model: VENDRE (107)*
(* = verb model number, not page number)

To conjugate a regular verb, you must add the appropriate verb ending to the appropriate tense stem. The stem for the Present, Imperfect, Past Historic and both Subjunctive tenses is the infinitive minus its ER, IR or RE ending; the stem for the Future and Conditional tenses is the whole infinitive in the 1st and 2nd Conjugations, and the infinitive minus its final E in the 3rd Conjugation.

For each conjugation, the following tables show
1) the verb endings for each tense
2) how these are added to the stem.
(*NB*: Pr. = Present; P. = Past)

1st Conjugation (1)

Tense	Endings					
Pres	e	es	e	ons	ez	ent
Imp	ais	ais	ait	ions	iez	aient
Fut	ai	as	a	ons	ez	ont
Cond	ais	as	ait	ions	iez	aient
P. Hist	ai	as	a	âmes	âtes	èrent
Pr. Subj	e	es	e	ions	iez	ent
P. Subj	asse	asses	ât	assions	assiez	assent

4

1st Conjugation (2)

	STEM	Pr	I	P H	Pr S	P S
je	**donn**	e	ais	ai	e	asse
tu	**donn**	es	ais	as	es	asses
il	**donn**	e	ait	a	e	ât
nous	**donn**	ons	ions	âmes	ions	assions
vous	**donn**	ez	iez	âtes	iez	assiez
ils	**donn**	ent	aient	èrent	ent	assent

	STEM	F	C
je	**donner**	ai	ais
tu	**donner**	as	ais
il	**donner**	a	ait
nous	**donner**	ons	ions
vous	**donner**	ez	iez
ils	**donner**	ont	aient

2nd Conjugation (1)

Tense	Endings					
Pres	is	is	it	issons	issez	issent
Imp	issais	issais	issait	issions	issiez	issaient
Fut	ai	as	a	ons	ez	ont
Cond	ais	ais	ait	ions	iez	aient
P. H.	is	is	it	îmes	îtes	irent
Pr. S.	isse	isses	isse	issions	issiez	issent
P. S.	isse	isses	ît	issions	issiez	issent

(2)

	STEM	Pr	I	P H	Pr S	P S
je	**fin**	is	issais	is	isse	isse
tu	**fin**	is	issais	is	isses	isses
il	**fin**	it	issait	it	isse	ît
nous	**fin**	issons	issions	îmes	issions	issions
vous	**fin**	issez	issiez	îtes	issiez	issiez
ils	**fin**	issent	issaient	irent	issent	issent

5

STEM		F	C
je	finir	ai	ais
tu	finir	as	ais
il	finir	a	ait
nous	finir	ons	ions
vous	finir	ez	iez
ils	finir	ont	aient

3rd Conjugation (1)

Tense	Endings					
Pres	s	s	—	ons	ez	ent
Imp	ais	ais	ait	ions	iez	aient
Fut	ai	as	a	ons	ez	ont
Cond	ais	ais	ait	ions	iez	aient
P. Hist	is	is	it	îmes	îtes	irent
Pr. Subj	e	es	e	ions	iez	ent
P. Subj	isse	isses	ît	issions	issiez	issent

(2)

STEM		Pr	I	P H	Pr S	P S
je	vend	s	ais	is	e	isse
tu	vend	s	ais	is	es	isses
il	vend		ait	it	e	ît
nous	vend	ons	ions	îmes	ions	issions
vous	vend	ez	iez	îtes	iez	issiez
ils	vend	ent	aient	irent	ent	issent

STEM		F	C
je	vendr	ai	ais
tu	vendr	as	ais
il	vendr	a	ait
nous	vendr	ons	ions
vous	vendr	ez	iez
ils	vendr	ont	aient

6

THE PRESENT PARTICIPLE

To form the present participle, add the following endings to the
infinitive minus its ER, IR or RE ending

   1st Conjugation ant   (donnant)
   2nd Conjugation issant (finissant)
   3rd Conjugation ant   (vendant)

With the exception of 'en', French uses an infinitive after
prepositions where English uses a present participle.
Thus: sans parler = without speaking
       après être parti = after having left
but: en faisant = while doing.

THE PAST PARTICIPLE

To form the past participle, add the following endings to the
infinitive minus its ER, IR or RE ending

   1st Conjugation é (donné)
   2nd Conjugation i (fini)
   3rd Conjugation u (vendu)

For agreement rules in Compound tenses, see p. 10.

THE IMPERATIVE

The Imperative is the same as the Present tense 'tu', 'nous' and
'vous' forms minus the subject pronouns: finis, allons,
commencez.
Exceptions
1) ER verbs and verbs like cueillir, ouvrir etc, which keep the
   's' ending of the 'tu' form only if it is immediately followed
   by y or en: avance, va; vas-y, cueilles-en.
2) avoir and être, whose Imperative forms are the same as the
   Present Subjunctive (minus the 's' of 'tu' form for avoir).
3) vouloir: veuille, veuillons, veuillez.
4) savoir: sache, sachons, sachez.
Affirmative/negative Imperative – pronoun object follows/
precedes verb: prends-le/ne le prends pas: asseyez-vous/ne vous
asseyez pas.

'REGULAR' SPELLING IRREGULARITIES

A number of spelling changes affect 1st Conjugation verbs. Such changes and when they occur are shown below. Verb types are divided according to their infinitive ending. We suggest that you use the table in conjunction with the numbered verb models indicated. C = consonant(s).

-eler/-eter (i: appeler 4/jeter 50; ii: acheter 1)	
either i) l → ll/t → tt	*before e, es, ent;*
or ii) e → è	*throughout Future and Conditional tenses*
-e+C+er (lever 52)	
e → è	*as above*
-éger (protéger 80)	*before e, es, ent;*
é → è; *see* **-ger**	*as for* **-ger**
-é+C+er (espérer 41)	
é → è	*before e, es, ent*
-oyer/-uyer (nettoyer 63)	*before e, es, ent;*
y → i	*throughout Future and Conditional tenses*
-ayer (i: payer 70; ii: as for nettoyer 63)	
either i) y retained throughout	
or ii) y → i	*as above*
-cer (commencer 15)	*when verb endings*
c → ç	*starting with a or o*
(to soften c)	*immediately follow c*
-ger (manger 54)	*when verb endings*
e retained	*starting with a or o*
(to soften g)	*immediately follow g*

8

GLOSSARY

You should familiarize yourself with the following descriptions of major verb categories.

transitive Taking a direct object

intransitive Used without a direct object

* A verb may be transitive in English yet intransitive in French (and vice versa):
he disobeyed the rules (transitive)
il a désobéi aux règles (intransitive)
he looked at his sister (intransitive)
il a regardé sa sœur (transitive)

reflexive Taking a reflexive pronoun (English: myself, ourselves etc; French: me, nous etc) which 'reflects' back to the subject

* 1) Not all verbs which are reflexive in French are reflexive in English
e.g. se coucher = to go to bed
2) The reflexive pronoun is sometimes optional in English
e.g. se laver = to wash (oneself)

reciprocal Taking a reciprocal pronoun which expresses mutual action or relation
e.g. ils se regardent = they look at each other
or one another

* Since the plural forms of Reciprocal and Reflexive verbs are identical, 'ils se regardent' might mean 'they look at themselves'. Always gauge the correct translation from the context.

auxiliary Used to conjugate verbs in their Compound tenses (see p. 10)

impersonal Used only in the 3rd person singular, to represent a neutral subject
e.g. il pleut = it's raining

9

COMPOUND TENSES: THE USE OF AUXILIARY VERBS

In Simple tenses, the verb is expressed in one word (e.g. donne, finira, vendions); in Compound tenses, the past participle is added to the appropriate tense of the auxiliary verbs avoir and être (e.g. a donné, aura fini, avions vendu). Most verbs are conjugated with avoir, but the être auxiliary is used with Reflexive and Reciprocal verbs, and when the verb is in the Passive Voice. (See note on Passive: p. 12)

The following intransitive verbs are also conjugated with être:

aller	revenir	passer*
venir	retourner*	rester
entrer*	rentrer*	devenir
sortir*	monter*	naître
arriver	descendre*	mourir
partir	tomber	

(* = conjugated with avoir when transitive)

Rules of Agreement for Past Participles

(a) The past participle of a verb conjugated with être agrees in number and gender with its subject.
Thus: elle est partie = she left
   elle s'est souvenue[1] = she remembered
   ([1]typical of verbs which are reflexive in form but whose
   pronouns have no true reflexive value)
Exceptions: 1) Reflexives 2) Reciprocals
    e.g.1) elle s'est lavée (transitive)
      elle s'est parlé (intransitive)
    2) ils se sont regardés (transitive)
     ils se sont parlé (intransitive)
  (Exceptions explained in (b))
(b) The past participle of a verb conjugated with avoir and of a transitive Reflexive or Reciprocal verb agrees in number

10

and gender with its direct object, provided the direct object precedes the verb; otherwise, the past participle remains invariable.

Thus: je les ai vendus = I sold them

elle s'est lavée = she washed

ils se sont regardés = they looked at each other

but: j'ai vendu les sacs = I sold the bags

elle s'est parlé = she talked to herself

(s' = indirect object)

ils se sont parlé = they talked to each other

(se = indirect object)

(*NB*: elle s'est lavé les mains = she washed her hands – no agreement since direct object (les mains) follows the verb and s' = indirect object)

Some intransitive verbs (e.g. coûter, peser etc) may be accompanied by a complement of price, weight etc. Do not mistake this for a direct object: the past participle remains invariable – 'les 5 F que ça m'a coûté = the 5 F it cost me'; 'les 3 kilos que le colis a pesé = the 3 kilos the parcel weighed'. Also invariable are the past participles of impersonal verbs – 'les accidents qu'il y a eu = the accidents there were'.

For verbal constructions of the type 'I saw her leave', 'she heard them being scolded' (verbs of perception), or 'he took us swimming', which are translated in French by a verb plus infinitive, the rules of agreement are as follows:

1) if the preceding direct object is the subject of the infinitive, the past participle agrees in number and gender with it:

je l'ai vue partir = I saw her leave

il nous a emmenés nager = he took us swimming

2) if the preceding direct object is the object of the infinitive, the past participle remains invariable:

elle les a entendu gronder

= she heard them being scolded.

In constructions such as 'laisser faire' where laisser is used in conjunction with an infinitive, the same rules apply:

    1) je les ai laissés tomber = I dropped them

    2) elle s'est laissé persuader = she let herself be persuaded.

When faire is used in this way, however, it contradicts the 1st rule: the past participle remains invariable in both cases:

    1) la femme qu'il a fait venir = the woman he sent for

    2) la montre qu'il a fait réparer = the watch he (has) had repaired.

The Passive Voice

A transitive verb is active when its subject performs the action (she disobeyed the rules) and passive when its subject receives the action (she was punished). In French, the passive is formed by adding the past participle to the appropriate tense of être: 'elle était punie = she was punished' (note agreement with subject).

    (*NB*: do not confuse a passive verb with an intransitive verb, which can only be used in the Active Voice –

        elle était allée = she had gone)

French does not use the passive as extensively as English, preferring

either 1) 'on': on m'a dit que ... = I was told that ...

or   2) a Reflexive verb with an inanimate subject:

        ce mot ne s'emploie plus = this word is no longer used.

Note

In the tables on the following pages these abbreviations are used.

qch	quelque chose
qn	quelqu'un
sb	somebody
sth	something

DEFECTIVE VERBS

Defective verbs have missing or obsolete parts. The forms shown below are those most likely to occur. Unless otherwise stated, the auxiliary verb (where applicable) is avoir.

1 Present Participle *2* Past Participle *3* Present *4* Imperfect
5 Future *6* Conditional *7* Past Historic *8* Present Subjunctive
9 Past Subjunctive

accroire en faire accroire
apparoir *3* il appert
béer *1* béant *3* il bée *4* il béait
choir (être) *2* chu *3* chois, chois, choit, choient *5* choirai *etc*
  6 choirais *etc* *7* il chut *9* il chût
déchoir *2* déchu *3* déchois, déchois, déchoit, déchoyons,
  déchoyez, déchoient *5* déchoirai *etc* *6* déchoirais *etc*
  7 déchus *etc* *8* déchoie *etc* *9* déchusse *etc*
échoir (être) *1* échéant *2* échu *3* il échoit *5* il échoira
  6 il échoirait *7* il échut *8* il échoie *9* il échût
faillir *1* faillant *2* failli *5* faillirai *etc* *6* faillirais *etc* *7* faillis *etc*
  NB: j'ai failli tomber = I nearly fell
gésir *1* gisant *3* gis, gis, gît, gisons, gisez, gisent *4* gisais *etc*
messeoir *1* messéant *3* il messied, ils messiéent
  6 il messiérait, ils messiéraient
oindre *1* oignant *2* oint *3* il oint *4* il oignait
ouïr *2* ouï
paître *1* paissant *3* pais, pais, paît, paissons, paissez, paissent
  4 paissais *etc* *5* paîtrai *etc* *6* paîtrais *etc* *8* paisse *etc*
poindre *2* point *3* il point *5* il poindra
repaître like **paître** but also has *2* repu *7* repus *etc* *9* repusse *etc*
seoir (= *to become*) *1* seyant *3* il sied, ils siéent *4* il seyait, ils
  seyaient *5* il siéra, ils siéront *6* il siérait, ils siéraient *8* il siée

13

1 acheter
to buy

also **congeler**
to freeze

PRESENT PARTICIPLE
achetant

déceler
to discover

PAST PARTICIPLE
acheté

geler
to freeze

PRESENT		IMPERFECT	
j'	achète	j'	achetais
tu	achètes	tu	achetais
il	achète	il	achetait
nous	achetons	nous	achetions
vous	achetez	vous	achetiez
ils	achètent	ils	achetaient

		FUTURE	
		j'	achèterai
		tu	achèteras
		il	achètera
		nous	achèterons
		vous	achèterez
		ils	achèteront

IMPERATIVE		CONDITIONAL	
	achète	j'	achèterais
	achetons	tu	achèterais
	achetez	il	achèterait
		nous	achèterions
		vous	achèteriez
		ils	achèteraient

14

haleter
to pant

peler
to peel

PAST HISTORIC		PRESENT SUBJUNCTIVE	
j'	achetai	j'	achète
tu	achetas	tu	achètes
il	acheta	il	achète
nous	achetâmes	nous	achetions
vous	achetâtes	vous	achetiez
ils	achetèrent	ils	achètent

PERFECT		PAST SUBJUNCTIVE	
j'	ai acheté	j'	achetasse
tu	as acheté	tu	achetasses
il	a acheté	il	achetât
nous	avons acheté	nous	achetassions
vous	avez acheté	vous	achetassiez
ils	ont acheté	ils	achetassent

CONSTRUCTIONS
acheter qch à qn   to buy sth from sb; to buy sth for sb
je le lui ai acheté   I bought it from him; I bought it for him
je le lui ai acheté 10 F   I bought it from him for 10 F

2 acquérir
to acquire

also **conquérir**
to conquer

PRESENT PARTICIPLE
acquérant

s'enquérir
to inquire

PAST PARTICIPLE
acquis

requérir
to require

PRESENT		IMPERFECT	
j'	acquiers	j'	acquérais
tu	acquiers	tu	acquérais
il	acquiert	il	acquérait
nous	acquérons	nous	acquérions
vous	acquérez	vous	acquériez
ils	acquièrent	ils	acquéraient

FUTURE	
j'	acquerrai
tu	acquerras
il	acquerra
nous	acquerrons
vous	acquerrez
ils	acquerront

IMPERATIVE		CONDITIONAL	
	acquiers	j'	acquerrais
	acquérons	tu	acquerrais
	acquérez	il	acquerrait
		nous	acquerrions
		vous	acquerriez
		ils	acquerraient

16

PAST HISTORIC		PRESENT SUBJUNCTIVE	
j'	acquis	j'	acquière
tu	acquis	tu	acquières
il	acquit	il	acquière
nous	acquîmes	nous	acquérions
vous	acquîtes	vous	acquériez
ils	acquirent	ils	acquièrent

PERFECT		PAST SUBJUNCTIVE	
j'	ai acquis	j'	acquisse
tu	as acquis	tu	acquisses
il	a acquis	il	acquît
nous	avons acquis	nous	acquissions
vous	avez acquis	vous	acquissiez
ils	ont acquis	ils	acquissent

CONSTRUCTIONS

acquérir de l'expérience to gain experience
acquérir de la valeur to go up in value
les mauvaises habitudes s'acquièrent facilement bad
habits are easily picked up

3 aller

to go

PRESENT PARTICIPLE
allant

PAST PARTICIPLE
allé

PRESENT		IMPERFECT	
je	**vais**	j'	**allais**
tu	**vas**	tu	**allais**
il	**va**	il	**allait**
nous	**allons**	nous	**allions**
vous	**allez**	vous	**alliez**
ils	**vont**	ils	**allaient**

		FUTURE	
		j'	**irai**
		tu	**iras**
		il	**ira**
		nous	**irons**
		vous	**irez**
		ils	**iront**

IMPERATIVE		CONDITIONAL	
	va	j'	**irais**
	allons	tu	**irais**
	allez	il	**irait**
		nous	**irions**
		vous	**iriez**
		ils	**iraient**

PAST HISTORIC		PRESENT SUBJUNCTIVE	
j'	allai	j'	aille
tu	allas	tu	ailles
il	alla	il	aille
nous	allâmes	nous	allions
vous	allâtes	vous	alliez
ils	allèrent	ils	aillent

PERFECT		PAST SUBJUNCTIVE	
je	suis allé	j'	allasse
tu	es allé	tu	allasses
il	est allé	il	allât
nous	sommes allés	nous	allassions
vous	êtes allé(s)	vous	allassiez
ils	sont allés	ils	allassent

CONSTRUCTIONS

aller faire qch to go and do sth
aller à qn to fit sb; to suit sb
comment allez-vous? – je vais bien/mal/mieux how are
you? – I'm well/unwell/better
s'en aller to go (away); to leave
allons-y! let's go!

4 appeler
to call

also **amonceler**
to pile up

PRESENT PARTICIPLE
appelant

épeler
to spell

PAST PARTICIPLE
appelé

jumeler
to twin

PRESENT			IMPERFECT	
j'	appelle		j'	appelais
tu	appelles		tu	appelais
il	appelle		il	appelait
nous	appelons		nous	appelions
vous	appelez		vous	appeliez
ils	appellent		ils	appelaient

FUTURE	
j'	appellerai
tu	appelleras
il	appellera
nous	appellerons
vous	appellerez
ils	appelleront

IMPERATIVE	CONDITIONAL	
appelle	j'	appellerais
appelons	tu	appellerais
appelez	il	appellerait
	nous	appellerions
	vous	appelleriez
	ils	appelleraient

20

rappeler
  to recall

renouveler
  to renew

PAST HISTORIC		PRESENT SUBJUNCTIVE	
j'	appelai	j'	appelle
tu	appelas	tu	appelles
il	appela	il	appelle
nous	appelâmes	nous	appelions
vous	appelâtes	vous	appeliez
ils	appelèrent	ils	appellent

PERFECT		PAST SUBJUNCTIVE	
j'	ai appelé	j'	appelasse
tu	as appelé	tu	appelasses
il	a appelé	il	appelât
nous	avons appelé	nous	appelassions
vous	avez appelé	vous	appelassiez
ils	ont appelé	ils	appelassent

CONSTRUCTIONS
comment vous appelez-vous? what's your name?
je m'appelle Suzanne my name is Suzanne
appeler qn à l'aide *or* **au secours** to call to sb for help
en appeler à to appeal to

5 apprendre
to learn

PRESENT PARTICIPLE
apprenant

PAST PARTICIPLE
appris

PRESENT		IMPERFECT	
j'	**apprends**	j'	**apprenais**
tu	**apprends**	tu	**apprenais**
il	**apprend**	il	**apprenait**
nous	**apprenons**	nous	**apprenions**
vous	**apprenez**	vous	**appreniez**
ils	**apprennent**	ils	**apprenaient**

FUTURE
j'	**apprendrai**
tu	**apprendras**
il	**apprendra**
nous	**apprendrons**
vous	**apprendrez**
ils	**apprendront**

IMPERATIVE
apprends
apprenons
apprenez

CONDITIONAL
j'	**apprendrais**
tu	**apprendrais**
il	**apprendrait**
nous	**apprendrions**
vous	**apprendriez**
ils	**apprendraient**

apprendre 5
to learn

apprendre à faire qch   to learn (how) to do sth

PAST HISTORIC		PRESENT SUBJUNCTIVE	
j'	appris	j'	apprenne
tu	appris	tu	apprennes
il	apprit	il	apprenne
nous	apprîmes	nous	apprenions
vous	apprîtes	vous	appreniez
ils	apprirent	ils	apprennent

PERFECT		PAST SUBJUNCTIVE	
j'	ai appris	j'	apprisse
tu	as appris	tu	apprisses
il	a appris	il	apprît
nous	avons appris	nous	apprissions
vous	avez appris	vous	apprissiez
ils	ont appris	ils	apprissent

CONSTRUCTIONS

apprendre à faire qch   to learn (how) to do sth
apprendre qch à qn   to teach sb sth; to tell sb sth
apprendre à qn à faire qch   to teach sb (how) to do sth
l'espagnol s'apprend facilement   Spanish is easy to learn

6 arriver
to arrive

PRESENT PARTICIPLE
arrivant

PAST PARTICIPLE
arrivé

PRESENT		IMPERFECT	
j'	arrive	j'	arrivais
tu	arrives	tu	arrivais
il	arrive	il	arrivait
nous	arrivons	nous	arrivions
vous	arrivez	vous	arriviez
ils	arrivent	ils	arrivaient

		FUTURE	
		j'	arriverai
		tu	arriveras
		il	arrivera
		nous	arriverons
		vous	arriverez
		ils	arriveront

IMPERATIVE		CONDITIONAL	
	arrive	j'	arriverais
	arrivons	tu	arriverais
	arrivez	il	arriverait
		nous	arriverions
		vous	arriveriez
		ils	arriveraient

PAST HISTORIC		PRESENT SUBJUNCTIVE	
j'	arrivai	j'	arrive
tu	arrivas	tu	arrives
il	arriva	il	arrive
nous	arrivâmes	nous	arrivions
vous	arrivâtes	vous	arriviez
ils	arrivèrent	ils	arrivent

PERFECT		PAST SUBJUNCTIVE	
je	suis arrivé	j'	arrivasse
tu	es arrivé	tu	arrivasses
il	est arrivé	il	arrivât
nous	sommes arrivés	nous	arrivassions
vous	êtes arrivé(s)	vous	arrivassiez
ils	sont arrivés	ils	arrivassent

CONSTRUCTIONS

arriver à faire qch   to succeed in doing sth
ça peut arriver   that may happen
il lui est arrivé un accident   he's had an accident
la neige lui arrivait (jusqu')aux genoux   the snow came
up to his knees

7 assaillir
to attack

PRESENT PARTICIPLE
assaillant

PAST PARTICIPLE
assailli

PRESENT		IMPERFECT	
j'	assaille	j'	assaillais
tu	assailles	tu	assaillais
il	assaille	il	assaillait
nous	assaillons	nous	assaillions
vous	assaillez	vous	assailliez
ils	assaillent	ils	assaillaient

		FUTURE	
		j'	assaillirai
		tu	assailliras
		il	assaillira
		nous	assaillirons
		vous	assaillirez
		ils	assailliront

IMPERATIVE		CONDITIONAL	
	assaille	j'	assaillirais
	assaillons	tu	assaillirais
	assaillez	il	assaillirait
		nous	assaillirions
		vous	assailliriez
		ils	assailliraient

PAST HISTORIC		PRESENT SUBJUNCTIVE	
j'	assaillis	j'	assaille
tu	assaillis	tu	assailles
il	assaillit	il	assaille
nous	assaillîmes	nous	assaillions
vous	assaillîtes	vous	assailliez
ils	assaillirent	ils	assaillent

PERFECT		PAST SUBJUNCTIVE	
j'	ai assailli	j'	assaillisse
tu	as assailli	tu	assaillisses
il	a assailli	il	assaillît
nous	avons assailli	nous	assaillissions
vous	avez assailli	vous	assaillissiez
ils	ont assailli	ils	assaillissent

CONSTRUCTIONS

on l'a assailli de questions   he was bombarded with
questions

8 s'asseoir
to sit down

PRESENT PARTICIPLE
s'asseyant

PAST PARTICIPLE
assis

PRESENT		IMPERFECT	
je	m'assieds	je	m'asseyais
tu	t'assieds	tu	t'asseyais
il	s'assied	il	s'asseyait
nous	nous asseyons	nous	nous asseyions
vous	vous asseyez	vous	vous asseyiez
ils	s'asseyent	ils	s'asseyaient

		FUTURE	
		je	m'assiérai
		tu	t'assiéras
		il	s'assiéra
		nous	nous assiérons
		vous	vous assiérez
		ils	s'assiéront

IMPERATIVE	CONDITIONAL	
assieds-toi	je	m'assiérais
asseyons-nous	tu	t'assiérais
asseyez-vous	il	s'assiérait
	nous	nous assiérions
	vous	vous assiériez
	ils	s'assiéraient

PAST HISTORIC		PRESENT SUBJUNCTIVE	
je	m'assis	je	m'asseye
tu	t'assis	tu	t'asseyes
il	s'assit	il	s'asseye
nous	nous assîmes	nous	nous asseyions
vous	vous assîtes	vous	vous asseyiez
ils	s'assirent	ils	s'asseyent

PERFECT		PAST SUBJUNCTIVE	
je	me suis assis	je	m'assisse
tu	t'es assis	tu	t'assisses
il	s'est assis	il	s'assît
nous	nous sommes assis	nous	nous assissions
vous	vous êtes assis	vous	vous assissiez
ils	se sont assis	ils	s'assissent

CONSTRUCTIONS

veuillez vous asseoir   please be seated
il s'est assis sur une chaise/par terre   he sat (down) on a chair/the floor
il est assis sur une chaise/par terre   he is sitting on a chair/the floor

29

9 attendre
to wait

PRESENT PARTICIPLE
attendant

PAST PARTICIPLE
attendu

PRESENT		IMPERFECT	
j'	attends	j'	attendais
tu	attends	tu	attendais
il	attend	il	attendait
nous	attendons	nous	attendions
vous	attendez	vous	attendiez
ils	attendent	ils	attendaient

FUTURE	
j'	attendrai
tu	attendras
il	attendra
nous	attendrons
vous	attendrez
ils	attendront

IMPERATIVE	CONDITIONAL	
attends	j'	attendrais
attendons	tu	attendrais
attendez	il	attendrait
	nous	attendrions
	vous	attendriez
	ils	attendraient

PAST HISTORIC		PRESENT SUBJUNCTIVE	
j'	attendis	j'	attende
tu	attendis	tu	attendes
il	attendit	il	attende
nous	attendîmes	nous	attendions
vous	attendîtes	vous	attendiez
ils	attendirent	ils	attendent

PERFECT		PAST SUBJUNCTIVE	
j'	ai attendu	j'	attendisse
tu	as attendu	tu	attendisses
il	a attendu	il	attendît
nous	avons attendu	nous	attendissions
vous	avez attendu	vous	attendissiez
ils	ont attendu	ils	attendissent

CONSTRUCTIONS

nous attendons qu'il parte we're waiting for him to leave
j'ai attendu 2 heures I waited (for) 2 hours
attends d'être plus grand wait till you're older
attendre qch de qn/qch to expect sth of sb/sth
s'attendre à qch/à faire to expect sth/to do

10 avoir
to have

PRESENT PARTICIPLE
ayant

PAST PARTICIPLE
eu

PRESENT		IMPERFECT
j'	**ai**	j' **avais**
tu	**as**	tu **avais**
il	**a**	il **avait**
nous	**avons**	nous **avions**
vous	**avez**	vous **aviez**
ils	**ont**	ils **avaient**

FUTURE
j'	**aurai**
tu	**auras**
il	**aura**
nous	**aurons**
vous	**aurez**
ils	**auront**

IMPERATIVE
aie
ayons
ayez

CONDITIONAL
j'	**aurais**
tu	**aurais**
il	**aurait**
nous	**aurions**
vous	**auriez**
ils	**auraient**

PAST HISTORIC		PRESENT SUBJUNCTIVE	
j'	eus	j'	aie
tu	eus	tu	aies
il	eut	il	ait
nous	eûmes	nous	ayons
vous	eûtes	vous	ayez
ils	eurent	ils	aient

PERFECT		PAST SUBJUNCTIVE	
j'	ai eu	j'	eusse
tu	as eu	tu	eusses
il	a eu	il	eût
nous	avons eu	nous	eussions
vous	avez eu	vous	eussiez
ils	ont eu	ils	eussent

CONSTRUCTIONS

j'ai des lettres à écrire I've got letters to write

quel âge avez-vous? – j'ai 10 ans how old are you? – I'm 10 (years old)

avoir faim/chaud/tort to be hungry/hot/wrong

il y a there is; there are

il y a 10 ans 10 years ago

11 battre

to beat

also **abattre**
to pull down

PRESENT PARTICIPLE
battant

combattre
to fight

PAST PARTICIPLE
battu

débattre
to discuss

PRESENT
je	bats
tu	bats
il	bat
nous	battons
vous	battez
ils	battent

IMPERFECT
je	battais
tu	battais
il	battait
nous	battions
vous	battiez
ils	battaient

FUTURE
je	battrai
tu	battras
il	battra
nous	battrons
vous	battrez
ils	battront

IMPERATIVE
bats
battons
battez

CONDITIONAL
je	battrais
tu	battrais
il	battrait
nous	battrions
vous	battriez
ils	battraient

rabattre
to pull down

PAST HISTORIC		PRESENT SUBJUNCTIVE	
je	battis	je	batte
tu	battis	tu	battes
il	battit	il	batte
nous	battîmes	nous	battions
vous	battîtes	vous	battiez
ils	battirent	ils	battent

PERFECT		PAST SUBJUNCTIVE	
j'	ai battu	je	battisse
tu	as battu	tu	battisses
il	a battu	il	battît
nous	avons battu	nous	battissions
vous	avez battu	vous	battissiez
ils	ont battu	ils	battissent

CONSTRUCTIONS
battre des mains to clap one's hands
l'oiseau battait des ailes the bird was flapping its wings
se battre to fight

12 boire
to drink

PRESENT PARTICIPLE
buvant

PAST PARTICIPLE
bu

PRESENT		IMPERFECT	
je	**bois**	je	**buvais**
tu	**bois**	tu	**buvais**
il	**boit**	il	**buvait**
nous	**buvons**	nous	**buvions**
vous	**buvez**	vous	**buviez**
ils	**boivent**	ils	**buvaient**

		FUTURE	
		je	**boirai**
		tu	**boiras**
		il	**boira**
		nous	**boirons**
		vous	**boirez**
		ils	**boiront**

IMPERATIVE		CONDITIONAL	
	bois	je	**boirais**
	buvons	tu	**boirais**
	buvez	il	**boirait**
		nous	**boirions**
		vous	**boiriez**
		ils	**boiraient**

boire 12
to drink

PAST HISTORIC		PRESENT SUBJUNCTIVE	
je	bus	je	boive
tu	bus	tu	boives
il	but	il	boive
nous	bûmes	nous	buvions
vous	bûtes	vous	buviez
ils	burent	ils	boivent

PERFECT		PAST SUBJUNCTIVE	
j'	ai bu	je	busse
tu	as bu	tu	busses
il	a bu	il	bût
nous	avons bu	nous	bussions
vous	avez bu	vous	bussiez
ils	ont bu	ils	bussent

CONSTRUCTIONS
boire un verre   to have a drink

13 bouillir
to boil

PRESENT PARTICIPLE
bouillant

PAST PARTICIPLE
bouilli

PRESENT		IMPERFECT	
je	bous	je	bouillais
tu	bous	tu	bouillais
il	bout	il	bouillait
nous	bouillons	nous	bouillions
vous	bouillez	vous	bouilliez
ils	bouillent	ils	bouillaient

		FUTURE	
		je	bouillirai
		tu	bouilliras
		il	bouillira
		nous	bouillirons
		vous	bouillirez
		ils	bouilliront

IMPERATIVE		CONDITIONAL	
	bous	je	bouillirais
	bouillons	tu	bouillirais
	bouillez	il	bouillirait
		nous	bouillirions
		vous	bouilliriez
		ils	bouilliraient

PAST HISTORIC		PRESENT SUBJUNCTIVE	
je	bouillis	je	bouille
tu	bouillis	tu	bouilles
il	bouillit	il	bouille
nous	bouillîmes	nous	bouillions
vous	bouillîtes	vous	bouilliez
ils	bouillirent	ils	bouillent

PERFECT		PAST SUBJUNCTIVE	
j'	ai bouilli	je	bouillisse
tu	as bouilli	tu	bouillisses
il	a bouilli	il	bouillît
nous	avons bouilli	nous	bouillissions
vous	avez bouilli	vous	bouillissiez
ils	ont bouilli	ils	bouillissent

CONSTRUCTIONS

faire bouillir de l'eau/des pommes de terre   to boil water/potatoes

bouillir de colère/d'impatience   to seethe with anger/impatience

14 clore
to shut

PRESENT PARTICIPLE
closant

PAST PARTICIPLE
clos

PRESENT		IMPERFECT	
je	clos	je	closais
tu	clos	tu	closais
il	clôt	il	closait
nous	closons	nous	closions
vous	closez	vous	closiez
ils	closent	ils	closaient

		FUTURE	
		je	clorai
		tu	cloras
		il	clora
		nous	clorons
		vous	clorez
		ils	cloront

IMPERATIVE		CONDITIONAL	
	not used	je	clorais
		tu	clorais
		il	clorait
		nous	clorions
		vous	cloriez
		ils	cloraient

PAST HISTORIC	PRESENT SUBJUNCTIVE
not used	je **close**
	tu **closes**
	il **close**
	nous **closions**
	vous **closiez**
	ils **closent**

PERFECT	PAST SUBJUNCTIVE
j' **ai clos**	*not used*
tu **as clos**	
il **a clos**	
nous **avons clos**	
vous **avez clos**	
ils **ont clos**	

CONSTRUCTIONS
le débat s'est clos sur cette remarque   the discussion
ended with that remark
clore le bec à qn   to shut sb up

15 commencer
to begin   *also* **annoncer**
to announce

PRESENT PARTICIPLE
commençant

avancer
to move forward

PAST PARTICIPLE
commencé

déplacer
to move

PRESENT		IMPERFECT	
je	commence	je	commençais
tu	commences	tu	commençais
il	commence	il	commençait
nous	commençons	nous	commencions
vous	commencez	vous	commenciez
ils	commencent	ils	commençaient

		FUTURE	
		je	commencerai
		tu	commenceras
		il	commencera
		nous	commencerons
		vous	commencerez
		ils	commenceront

IMPERATIVE		CONDITIONAL	
	commence	je	commencerais
	commençons	tu	commencerais
	commencez	il	commencerait
		nous	commencerions
		vous	commenceriez
		ils	commenceraient

effacer
to erase

lancer
to throw

PAST HISTORIC		PRESENT SUBJUNCTIVE	
je	commençai	je	commence
tu	commenças	tu	commences
il	commença	il	commence
nous	commençâmes	nous	commencions
vous	commençâtes	vous	commenciez
ils	commencèrent	ils	commencent

PERFECT		PAST SUBJUNCTIVE	
j'	ai commencé	je	commençasse
tu	as commencé	tu	commençasses
il	a commencé	il	commençât
nous	avons commencé	nous	commençassions
vous	avez commencé	vous	commençassiez
ils	ont commencé	ils	commençassent

CONSTRUCTIONS
commencer à *or* **de faire**   to begin to do
commencer par qch   to begin with sth
commencer par faire qch   to begin by doing sth
il commence à pleuvoir   it's beginning to rain

16 comprendre
to understand

PRESENT PARTICIPLE
comprenant

PAST PARTICIPLE
compris

PRESENT	IMPERFECT
je **comprends**	je **comprenais**
tu **comprends**	tu **comprenais**
il **comprend**	il **comprenait**
nous **comprenons**	nous **comprenions**
vous **comprenez**	vous **compreniez**
ils **comprennent**	ils **comprenaient**

FUTURE
je **comprendrai**
tu **comprendras**
il **comprendra**
nous **comprendrons**
vous **comprendrez**
ils **comprendront**

IMPERATIVE	CONDITIONAL
comprends	je **comprendrais**
comprenons	tu **comprendrais**
comprenez	il **comprendrait**
	nous **comprendrions**
	vous **comprendriez**
	ils **comprendraient**

to understand

PAST HISTORIC		PRESENT SUBJUNCTIVE	
je	compris	je	comprenne
tu	compris	tu	comprennes
il	comprit	il	comprenne
nous	comprîmes	nous	comprenions
vous	comprîtes	vous	compreniez
ils	comprirent	ils	comprennent

PERFECT		PAST SUBJUNCTIVE	
j'	ai compris	je	comprisse
tu	as compris	tu	comprisses
il	a compris	il	comprît
nous	avons compris	nous	comprissions
vous	avez compris	vous	comprissiez
ils	ont compris	ils	comprissent

CONSTRUCTIONS

la maison comprend 10 pièces   the house comprises 10 rooms

mal comprendre   to misunderstand

service compris   service charge included

100 F y compris l'électricité *or* **l'électricité y comprise**   100 F including electricity

17 conclure
to conclude

also **exclure**
to exclude

PRESENT PARTICIPLE
concluant

PAST PARTICIPLE
conclu

PRESENT		IMPERFECT	
je	conclus	je	concluais
tu	conclus	tu	concluais
il	conclut	il	concluait
nous	concluons	nous	concluions
vous	concluez	vous	concluiez
ils	concluent	ils	concluaient

		FUTURE	
		je	conclurai
		tu	concluras
		il	conclura
		nous	conclurons
		vous	conclurez
		ils	concluront

IMPERATIVE		CONDITIONAL	
	conclus	je	conclurais
	concluons	tu	conclurais
	concluez	il	conclurait
		nous	conclurions
		vous	concluriez
		ils	concluraient

to conclude

PAST HISTORIC	PRESENT SUBJUNCTIVE
je **conclus**	je **conclue**
tu **conclus**	tu **conclues**
il **conclut**	il **conclue**
nous **conclûmes**	nous **concluions**
vous **conclûtes**	vous **concluiez**
ils **conclurent**	ils **concluent**

PERFECT	PAST SUBJUNCTIVE
j' **ai conclu**	je **conclusse**
tu **as conclu**	tu **conclusses**
il **a conclu**	il **conclût**
nous **avons conclu**	nous **conclussions**
vous **avez conclu**	vous **conclussiez**
ils **ont conclu**	ils **conclussent**

CONSTRUCTIONS

marché conclu! it's a deal!

j'en ai conclu qu'il était parti I concluded that he had gone

ils ont conclu à son innocence they concluded that he was innocent

47

18 conduire
to lead

also **éconduire**
to dismiss

PRESENT PARTICIPLE
conduisant

PAST PARTICIPLE
conduit

PRESENT		IMPERFECT	
je	conduis	je	conduisais
tu	conduis	tu	conduisais
il	conduit	il	conduisait
nous	conduisons	nous	conduisions
vous	conduisez	vous	conduisiez
ils	conduisent	ils	conduisaient

		FUTURE	
		je	conduirai
		tu	conduiras
		il	conduira
		nous	conduirons
		vous	conduirez
		ils	conduiront

IMPERATIVE		CONDITIONAL	
	conduis	je	conduirais
	conduisons	tu	conduirais
	conduisez	il	conduirait
		nous	conduirions
		vous	conduiriez
		ils	conduiraient

PAST HISTORIC		PRESENT SUBJUNCTIVE	
je	conduisis	je	conduise
tu	conduisis	tu	conduises
il	conduisit	il	conduise
nous	conduisîmes	nous	conduisions
vous	conduisîtes	vous	conduisiez
ils	conduisirent	ils	conduisent

PERFECT		PAST SUBJUNCTIVE	
j'	ai conduit	je	conduisisse
tu	as conduit	tu	conduisisses
il	a conduit	il	conduisît
nous	avons conduit	nous	conduisissions
vous	avez conduit	vous	conduisissiez
ils	ont conduit	ils	conduisissent

CONSTRUCTIONS

conduire qn quelque part   to take sb somewhere; to drive sb somewhere

conduire qn à faire qch   to lead sb to do sth

cet escalier conduit au toit   these stairs lead (up) to the roof

se conduire   to behave (oneself)

19 connaître
to know

also **méconnaître**
to be unaware of

PRESENT PARTICIPLE
connaissant

reconnaître
to recognize

PAST PARTICIPLE
connu

PRESENT		IMPERFECT	
je	connais	je	connaissais
tu	connais	tu	connaissais
il	connaît	il	connaissait
nous	connaissons	nous	connaissions
vous	connaissez	vous	connaissiez
ils	connaissent	ils	connaissaient

		FUTURE	
		je	connaîtrai
		tu	connaîtras
		il	connaîtra
		nous	connaîtrons
		vous	connaîtrez
		ils	connaîtront

IMPERATIVE		CONDITIONAL	
	connais	je	connaîtrais
	connaissons	tu	connaîtrais
	connaissez	il	connaîtrait
		nous	connaîtrions
		vous	connaîtriez
		ils	connaîtraient

50

PAST HISTORIC		PRESENT SUBJUNCTIVE	
je	connus	je	connaisse
tu	connus	tu	connaisses
il	connut	il	connaisse
nous	connûmes	nous	connaissions
vous	connûtes	vous	connaissiez
ils	connurent	ils	connaissent
PERFECT		PAST SUBJUNCTIVE	
j'	ai connu	je	connusse
tu	as connu	tu	connusses
il	a connu	il	connût
nous	avons connu	nous	connussions
vous	avez connu	vous	connussiez
ils	ont connu	ils	connussent

CONSTRUCTIONS

connaître qn de vue/nom to know sb by sight/name
il connaît bien la littérature anglaise he's very familiar
with English literature
faire connaître qn à qn to introduce sb to sb
se faire connaître to make a name for oneself; to
introduce oneself

20 coudre
to sew

PRESENT PARTICIPLE
cousant

PAST PARTICIPLE
cousu

PRESENT		IMPERFECT	
je	couds	je	cousais
tu	couds	tu	cousais
il	coud	il	cousait
nous	cousons	nous	cousions
vous	cousez	vous	cousiez
ils	cousent	ils	cousaient

		FUTURE	
		je	coudrai
		tu	coudras
		il	coudra
		nous	coudrons
		vous	coudrez
		ils	coudront

IMPERATIVE		CONDITIONAL	
	couds	je	coudrais
	cousons	tu	coudrais
	cousez	il	coudrait
		nous	coudrions
		vous	coudriez
		ils	coudraient

PAST HISTORIC		PRESENT SUBJUNCTIVE	
je	cousis	je	couse
tu	cousis	tu	couses
il	cousit	il	couse
nous	cousîmes	nous	cousions
vous	cousîtes	vous	cousiez
ils	cousirent	ils	cousent

PERFECT		PAST SUBJUNCTIVE	
j'	ai cousu	je	cousisse
tu	as cousu	tu	cousisses
il	a cousu	il	cousît
nous	avons cousu	nous	cousissions
vous	avez cousu	vous	cousissiez
ils	ont cousu	ils	cousissent

CONSTRUCTIONS

coudre un bouton à une veste   to sew a button on a jacket

21 courir
to run

also **accourir**
to rush

PRESENT PARTICIPLE
courant

concourir
to compete

PAST PARTICIPLE
couru

parcourir
to go through

PRESENT		IMPERFECT	
je	cours	je	courais
tu	cours	tu	courais
il	court	il	courait
nous	courons	nous	courions
vous	courez	vous	couriez
ils	courent	ils	couraient

		FUTURE	
		je	courrai
		tu	courras
		il	courra
		nous	courrons
		vous	courrez
		ils	courront

IMPERATIVE	CONDITIONAL	
cours	je	courrais
courons	tu	courrais
courez	il	courrait
	nous	courrions
	vous	courriez
	ils	courraient

secourir
to rescue

PAST HISTORIC	PRESENT SUBJUNCTIVE
je **courus**	je **coure**
tu **courus**	tu **coures**
il **courut**	il **coure**
nous **courûmes**	nous **courions**
vous **courûtes**	vous **couriez**
ils **coururent**	ils **courent**

PERFECT	PAST SUBJUNCTIVE
j' **ai couru**	je **courusse**
tu **as couru**	tu **courusses**
il **a couru**	il **courût**
nous **avons couru**	nous **courussions**
vous **avez couru**	vous **courussiez**
ils **ont couru**	ils **courussent**

CONSTRUCTIONS

courir faire qch to rush and do sth
courir à toutes jambes to run as fast as one's legs can carry one
le bruit court que … the rumour is going round that …
courir le risque de to run the risk of

22 couvrir
to cover

also **recouvrir**
to re-cover

PRESENT PARTICIPLE
couvrant

PAST PARTICIPLE
couvert

PRESENT		IMPERFECT	
je	couvre	je	couvrais
tu	couvres	tu	couvrais
il	couvre	il	couvrait
nous	couvrons	nous	couvrions
vous	couvrez	vous	couvriez
ils	couvrent	ils	couvraient

		FUTURE	
		je	couvrirai
		tu	couvriras
		il	couvrira
		nous	couvrirons
		vous	couvrirez
		ils	couvriront

IMPERATIVE		CONDITIONAL	
	couvre	je	couvrirais
	couvrons	tu	couvrirais
	couvrez	il	couvrirait
		nous	couvririons
		vous	couvririez
		ils	couvriraient

PAST HISTORIC		PRESENT SUBJUNCTIVE	
je	couvris	je	couvre
tu	couvris	tu	couvres
il	couvrit	il	couvre
nous	couvrîmes	nous	couvrions
vous	couvrîtes	vous	couvriez
ils	couvrirent	ils	couvrent

PERFECT		PAST SUBJUNCTIVE	
j'	ai couvert	je	couvrisse
tu	as couvert	tu	couvrisses
il	a couvert	il	couvrît
nous	avons couvert	nous	couvrissions
vous	avez couvert	vous	couvrissiez
ils	ont couvert	ils	couvrissent

CONSTRUCTIONS

la voiture nous a couverts de boue   the car covered us in mud

couvrir qn de cadeaux   to shower sb with gifts

elle s'est couvert le visage des mains   she covered her face with her hands

couvrez-vous bien!   wrap up well!

23 craindre
to fear

also **contraindre**
to compel

PRESENT PARTICIPLE
craignant

plaindre
to pity

PAST PARTICIPLE
craint

PRESENT		IMPERFECT	
je	crains	je	craignais
tu	crains	tu	craignais
il	craint	il	craignait
nous	craignons	nous	craignions
vous	craignez	vous	craigniez
ils	craignent	ils	craignaient

		FUTURE	
		je	craindrai
		tu	craindras
		il	craindra
		nous	craindrons
		vous	craindrez
		ils	craindront

IMPERATIVE		CONDITIONAL	
	crains	je	craindrais
	craignons	tu	craindrais
	craignez	il	craindrait
		nous	craindrions
		vous	craindriez
		ils	craindraient

PAST HISTORIC		PRESENT SUBJUNCTIVE	
je	craignis	je	craigne
tu	craignis	tu	craignes
il	craignit	il	craigne
nous	craignîmes	nous	craignions
vous	craignîtes	vous	craigniez
ils	craignirent	ils	craignent

PERFECT		PAST SUBJUNCTIVE	
j'	ai craint	je	craignisse
tu	as craint	tu	craignisses
il	a craint	il	craignît
nous	avons craint	nous	craignissions
vous	avez craint	vous	craignissiez
ils	ont craint	ils	craignissent

CONSTRUCTIONS

ne craignez rien don't be afraid

craindre de faire qch to be afraid of doing sth

ces plantes craignent la chaleur these plants dislike heat

24 créer
to create   *also* **agréer**
               to accept

PRESENT PARTICIPLE
créant   **maugréer**
               to grumble

PAST PARTICIPLE
créé   **procréer**
               to procreate

PRESENT		IMPERFECT	
je	crée	je	créais
tu	crées	tu	créais
il	crée	il	créait
nous	créons	nous	créions
vous	créez	vous	créiez
ils	créent	ils	créaient

		FUTURE	
		je	créerai
		tu	créeras
		il	créera
		nous	créerons
		vous	créerez
		ils	créeront

IMPERATIVE		CONDITIONAL	
	crée	je	créerais
	créons	tu	créerais
	créez	il	créerait
		nous	créerions
		vous	créeriez
		ils	créeraient

PAST HISTORIC		PRESENT SUBJUNCTIVE	
je	créai	je	crée
tu	créas	tu	crées
il	créa	il	crée
nous	créâmes	nous	créions
vous	créâtes	vous	créiez
ils	créèrent	ils	créent

PERFECT		PAST SUBJUNCTIVE	
j'	ai créé	je	créasse
tu	as créé	tu	créasses
il	a créé	il	créât
nous	avons créé	nous	créassions
vous	avez créé	vous	créassiez
ils	ont créé	ils	créassent

CONSTRUCTIONS

il nous a créé des ennuis   he's caused us problems
il s'est créé une clientèle   he has built up custom

25 crier
to shout

also **amplifier**
to amplify

PRESENT PARTICIPLE
criant

associer
to associate

PAST PARTICIPLE
crié

copier
to copy

PRESENT
je	crie
tu	cries
il	crie
nous	crions
vous	criez
ils	crient

IMPERFECT
je	criais
tu	criais
il	criait
nous	criions
vous	criiez
ils	criaient

FUTURE
je	crierai
tu	crieras
il	criera
nous	crierons
vous	crierez
ils	crieront

IMPERATIVE
	crie
	crions
	criez

CONDITIONAL
je	crierais
tu	crierais
il	crierait
nous	crierions
vous	crieriez
ils	crieraient

étudier
to study

marier
to marry

PAST HISTORIC		PRESENT SUBJUNCTIVE	
je	criai	je	crie
tu	crias	tu	cries
il	cria	il	crie
nous	criâmes	nous	criions
vous	criâtes	vous	criiez
ils	crièrent	ils	crient

PERFECT		PAST SUBJUNCTIVE	
j'	ai crié	je	criasse
tu	as crié	tu	criasses
il	a crié	il	criât
nous	avons crié	nous	criassions
vous	avez crié	vous	criassiez
ils	ont crié	ils	criassent

CONSTRUCTIONS

crier à tue-tête   to shout one's head off
crier contre *or* **après qn**   to nag (at) sb
crier à qn de faire qch   to shout at sb to do sth
crier qch sur les toits   to proclaim sth from the rooftops
crier au secours   to shout for help

26 croire
to believe

PRESENT PARTICIPLE
croyant

PAST PARTICIPLE
cru

PRESENT		IMPERFECT	
je	crois	je	croyais
tu	crois	tu	croyais
il	croit	il	croyait
nous	croyons	nous	croyions
vous	croyez	vous	croyiez
ils	croient	ils	croyaient

		FUTURE	
		je	croirai
		tu	croiras
		il	croira
		nous	croirons
		vous	croirez
		ils	croiront

IMPERATIVE		CONDITIONAL	
	crois	je	croirais
	croyons	tu	croirais
	croyez	il	croirait
		nous	croirions
		vous	croiriez
		ils	croiraient

PAST HISTORIC	PRESENT SUBJUNCTIVE
je crus	je croie
tu crus	tu croies
il crut	il croie
nous crûmes	nous croyions
vous crûtes	vous croyiez
ils crurent	ils croient

PERFECT	PAST SUBJUNCTIVE
j' ai cru	je crusse
tu as cru	tu crusses
il a cru	il crût
nous avons cru	nous crussions
vous avez cru	vous crussiez
ils ont cru	ils crussent

CONSTRUCTIONS

croire aux fantômes/en Dieu to believe in ghosts/God
on l'a cru mort he was presumed (to be) dead
elle croyait avoir perdu son sac she thought she had lost her bag
je crois que oui I think so, I think we will *etc*

27 croître
to grow

PRESENT PARTICIPLE
croissant

PAST PARTICIPLE
crû (*NB*: **crue, crus, crues**)

PRESENT		IMPERFECT	
je	crois	je	croissais
tu	crois	tu	croissais
il	croît	il	croissait
nous	croissons	nous	croissions
vous	croissez	vous	croissiez
ils	croissent	ils	croissaient

		FUTURE	
		je	croîtrai
		tu	croîtras
		il	croîtra
		nous	croîtrons
		vous	croîtrez
		ils	croîtront

IMPERATIVE		CONDITIONAL	
	crois	je	croîtrais
	croissons	tu	croîtrais
	croissez	il	croîtrait
		nous	croîtrions
		vous	croîtriez
		ils	croîtraient

PAST HISTORIC		PRESENT SUBJUNCTIVE	
je	**crûs**	je	**croisse**
tu	**crûs**	tu	**croisses**
il	**crût**	il	**croisse**
nous	**crûmes**	nous	**croissions**
vous	**crûtes**	vous	**croissiez**
ils	**crûrent**	ils	**croissent**

PERFECT		PAST SUBJUNCTIVE	
j'	**ai crû**	je	**crûsse**
tu	**as crû**	tu	**crûsses**
il	**a crû**	il	**crût**
nous	**avons crû**	nous	**crûssions**
vous	**avez crû**	vous	**crûssiez**
ils	**ont crû**	ils	**crûssent**

CONSTRUCTIONS

croître en beauté/nombre   to grow in beauty/number
les jours croissent   the days are getting longer

28 cueillir
to pick

also **accueillir**
to welcome

PRESENT PARTICIPLE
cueillant

recueillir
to collect

PAST PARTICIPLE
cueilli

PRESENT		IMPERFECT	
je	**cueille**	je	**cueillais**
tu	**cueilles**	tu	**cueillais**
il	**cueille**	il	**cueillait**
nous	**cueillons**	nous	**cueillions**
vous	**cueillez**	vous	**cueilliez**
ils	**cueillent**	ils	**cueillaient**

FUTURE
je	**cueillerai**
tu	**cueilleras**
il	**cueillera**
nous	**cueillerons**
vous	**cueillerez**
ils	**cueilleront**

IMPERATIVE
cueille
cueillons
cueillez

CONDITIONAL
je	**cueillerais**
tu	**cueillerais**
il	**cueillerait**
nous	**cueillerions**
vous	**cueilleriez**
ils	**cueilleraient**

PAST HISTORIC		PRESENT SUBJUNCTIVE	
je	cueillis	je	cueille
tu	cueillis	tu	cueilles
il	cueillit	il	cueille
nous	cueillîmes	nous	cueillions
vous	cueillîtes	vous	cueilliez
ils	cueillirent	ils	cueillent

PERFECT		PAST SUBJUNCTIVE	
j'	ai cueilli	je	cueillisse
tu	as cueilli	tu	cueillisses
il	a cueilli	il	cueillît
nous	avons cueilli	nous	cueillissions
vous	avez cueilli	vous	cueillissiez
ils	ont cueilli	ils	cueillissent

CONSTRUCTIONS
cueillir qn à froid   to catch sb off guard

29 cuire
to cook

also **construire**
to build

PRESENT PARTICIPLE
cuisant

instruire
to teach

PAST PARTICIPLE
cuit

produire
to produce

PRESENT		IMPERFECT	
je	cuis	je	cuisais
tu	cuis	tu	cuisais
il	cuit	il	cuisait
nous	cuisons	nous	cuisions
vous	cuisez	vous	cuisiez
ils	cuisent	ils	cuisaient

		FUTURE	
		je	cuirai
		tu	cuiras
		il	cuira
		nous	cuirons
		vous	cuirez
		ils	cuiront

IMPERATIVE		CONDITIONAL	
	cuis	je	cuirais
	cuisons	tu	cuirais
	cuisez	il	cuirait
		nous	cuirions
		vous	cuiriez
		ils	cuiraient

70

réduire
to reduce

séduire
to charm

PAST HISTORIC		PRESENT SUBJUNCTIVE	
je	cuisis	je	cuise
tu	cuisis	tu	cuises
il	cuisit	il	cuise
nous	cuisîmes	nous	cuisions
vous	cuisîtes	vous	cuisiez
ils	cuisirent	ils	cuisent

PERFECT		PAST SUBJUNCTIVE	
j'	ai cuit	je	cuisisse
tu	as cuit	tu	cuisisses
il	a cuit	il	cuisît
nous	avons cuit	nous	cuisissions
vous	avez cuit	vous	cuisissiez
ils	ont cuit	ils	cuisissent

CONSTRUCTIONS

cuire au gaz/à l'électricité   to cook with gas/by electricity
cuire au four   to bake; to roast
cuire à la vapeur   to steam
cuire à feu doux   to cook gently
bien cuit   well done

30 découvrir
to discover

PRESENT PARTICIPLE
découvrant

PAST PARTICIPLE
découvert

PRESENT		IMPERFECT	
je	**découvre**	je	**découvrais**
tu	**découvres**	tu	**découvrais**
il	**découvre**	il	**découvrait**
nous	**découvrons**	nous	**découvrions**
vous	**découvrez**	vous	**découvriez**
ils	**découvrent**	ils	**découvraient**

FUTURE
je	**découvrirai**
tu	**découvriras**
il	**découvrira**
nous	**découvrirons**
vous	**découvrirez**
ils	**découvriront**

IMPERATIVE
découvre
découvrons
découvrez

CONDITIONAL
je	**découvrirais**
tu	**découvrirais**
il	**découvrirait**
nous	**découvririons**
vous	**découvririez**
ils	**découvriraient**

72

to discover

PAST HISTORIC		PRESENT SUBJUNCTIVE	
je	découvris	je	découvre
tu	découvris	tu	découvres
il	découvrit	il	découvre
nous	découvrîmes	nous	découvrions
vous	découvrîtes	vous	découvriez
ils	découvrirent	ils	découvrent

PERFECT		PAST SUBJUNCTIVE	
j'	ai découvert	je	découvrisse
tu	as découvert	tu	découvrisses
il	a découvert	il	découvrît
nous	avons découvert	nous	découvrissions
vous	avez découvert	vous	découvrissiez
ils	ont découvert	ils	découvrissent

CONSTRUCTIONS

il craint d'être découvert   he's afraid of being found out
une robe qui découvre les épaules   a dress which reveals
the shoulders
se découvrir   to take off one's hat; to undress

31 descendre
to go down

PRESENT PARTICIPLE
descendant

PAST PARTICIPLE
descendu

PRESENT		IMPERFECT	
je	descends	je	descendais
tu	descends	tu	descendais
il	descend	il	descendait
nous	descendons	nous	descendions
vous	descendez	vous	descendiez
ils	descendent	ils	descendaient

		FUTURE	
		je	descendrai
		tu	descendras
		il	descendra
		nous	descendrons
		vous	descendrez
		ils	descendront

IMPERATIVE	CONDITIONAL	
descends	je	descendrais
descendons	tu	descendrais
descendez	il	descendrait
	nous	descendrions
	vous	descendriez
	ils	descendraient

PAST HISTORIC		PRESENT SUBJUNCTIVE	
je	**descendis**	je	**descende**
tu	**descendis**	tu	**descendes**
il	**descendit**	il	**descende**
nous	**descendîmes**	nous	**descendions**
vous	**descendîtes**	vous	**descendiez**
ils	**descendirent**	ils	**descendent**

PERFECT		PAST SUBJUNCTIVE	
je	**suis descendu**	je	**descendisse**
tu	**es descendu**	tu	**descendisses**
il	**est descendu**	il	**descendît**
nous	**sommes descendus**	nous	**descendissions**
vous	**êtes descendu(s)**	vous	**descendissiez**
ils	**sont descendus**	ils	**descendissent**

CONSTRUCTIONS

descendre de voiture/du train/de bicyclette   to get out of the car/off the train/off one's bicycle

sa jupe lui descend jusqu'aux chevilles   her skirt comes down to her ankles

il a descendu la valise   he took the case down

32 détruire
to destroy

PRESENT PARTICIPLE
détruisant

PAST PARTICIPLE
détruit

PRESENT		IMPERFECT	
je	détruis	je	détruisais
tu	détruis	tu	détruisais
il	détruit	il	détruisait
nous	détruisons	nous	détruisions
vous	détruisez	vous	détruisiez
ils	détruisent	ils	détruisaient

		FUTURE	
		je	détruirai
		tu	détruiras
		il	détruira
		nous	détruirons
		vous	détruirez
		ils	détruiront

IMPERATIVE		CONDITIONAL	
	détruis	je	détruirais
	détruisons	tu	détruirais
	détruisez	il	détruirait
		nous	détruirions
		vous	détruiriez
		ils	détruiraient

PAST HISTORIC		PRESENT SUBJUNCTIVE	
je	détruisis	je	détruise
tu	détruisis	tu	détruises
il	détruisit	il	détruise
nous	détruisîmes	nous	détruisions
vous	détruisîtes	vous	détruisiez
ils	détruisirent	ils	détruisent

PERFECT		PAST SUBJUNCTIVE	
j'	ai détruit	je	détruisisse
tu	as détruit	tu	détruisisses
il	a détruit	il	détruisît
nous	avons détruit	nous	détruisissions
vous	avez détruit	vous	détruisissiez
ils	ont détruit	ils	détruisissent

CONSTRUCTIONS
détruire par le feu   to destroy by fire

33 devenir
to become

PRESENT PARTICIPLE
devenant

PAST PARTICIPLE
devenu

PRESENT		IMPERFECT	
je	**deviens**	je	**devenais**
tu	**deviens**	tu	**devenais**
il	**devient**	il	**devenait**
nous	**devenons**	nous	**devenions**
vous	**devenez**	vous	**deveniez**
ils	**deviennent**	ils	**devenaient**

		FUTURE	
		je	**deviendrai**
		tu	**deviendras**
		il	**deviendra**
		nous	**deviendrons**
		vous	**deviendrez**
		ils	**deviendront**

IMPERATIVE		CONDITIONAL	
	deviens	je	**deviendrais**
	devenons	tu	**deviendrais**
	devenez	il	**deviendrait**
		nous	**deviendrions**
		vous	**deviendriez**
		ils	**deviendraient**

78

PAST HISTORIC		PRESENT SUBJUNCTIVE	
je	devins	je	devienne
tu	devins	tu	deviennes
il	devint	il	devienne
nous	devînmes	nous	devenions
vous	devîntes	vous	deveniez
ils	devinrent	ils	deviennent

PERFECT		PAST SUBJUNCTIVE	
je	suis devenu	je	devinsse
tu	es devenu	tu	devinsses
il	est devenu	il	devînt
nous	sommes devenus	nous	devinssions
vous	êtes devenu(s)	vous	devinssiez
ils	sont devenus	ils	devinssent

CONSTRUCTIONS

devenir médecin/professeur to become a doctor/a teacher

devenir vieux/grand to get old/tall

qu'est-il devenu? what has become of him?

il devient de plus en plus agressif he's growing increasingly aggressive

34 devoir
to have to; to owe

PRESENT PARTICIPLE
devant

PAST PARTICIPLE
dû (*NB*: **due, dus, dues**)

PRESENT		IMPERFECT	
je	**dois**	je	**devais**
tu	**dois**	tu	**devais**
il	**doit**	il	**devait**
nous	**devons**	nous	**devions**
vous	**devez**	vous	**deviez**
ils	**doivent**	ils	**devaient**

		FUTURE	
		je	**devrai**
		tu	**devras**
		il	**devra**
		nous	**devrons**
		vous	**devrez**
		ils	**devront**

IMPERATIVE		CONDITIONAL	
	dois	je	**devrais**
	devons	tu	**devrais**
	devez	il	**devrait**
		nous	**devrions**
		vous	**devriez**
		ils	**devraient**

to have to; to owe

PAST HISTORIC		PRESENT SUBJUNCTIVE	
je	dus	je	doive
tu	dus	tu	doives
il	dut	il	doive
nous	dûmes	nous	devions
vous	dûtes	vous	deviez
ils	durent	ils	doivent
PERFECT		PAST SUBJUNCTIVE	
j'	ai dû	je	dusse
tu	as dû	tu	dusses
il	a dû	il	dût
nous	avons dû	nous	dussions
vous	avez dû	vous	dussiez
ils	ont dû	ils	dussent

CONSTRUCTIONS
devoir qch à qn   to owe sb sth
devoir faire qch   to have to do sth
il doit arriver ce soir   he is due (to arrive) tonight
il a dû s'égarer   he must have got lost
ceci est dû à ...   this is due to ...

35 dire
to say

PRESENT PARTICIPLE
disant

PAST PARTICIPLE
dit

PRESENT		IMPERFECT	
je	**dis**	je	**disais**
tu	**dis**	tu	**disais**
il	**dit**	il	**disait**
nous	**disons**	nous	**disions**
vous	**dites**	vous	**disiez**
ils	**disent**	ils	**disaient**

		FUTURE	
		je	**dirai**
		tu	**diras**
		il	**dira**
		nous	**dirons**
		vous	**direz**
		ils	**diront**

IMPERATIVE		CONDITIONAL	
	dis	je	**dirais**
	disons	tu	**dirais**
	dites	il	**dirait**
		nous	**dirions**
		vous	**diriez**
		ils	**diraient**

PAST HISTORIC		PRESENT SUBJUNCTIVE	
je	**dis**	je	**dise**
tu	**dis**	tu	**dises**
il	**dit**	il	**dise**
nous	**dîmes**	nous	**disions**
vous	**dîtes**	vous	**disiez**
ils	**dirent**	ils	**disent**

PERFECT		PAST SUBJUNCTIVE	
j'	**ai dit**	je	**disse**
tu	**as dit**	tu	**disses**
il	**a dit**	il	**dît**
nous	**avons dit**	nous	**dissions**
vous	**avez dit**	vous	**dissiez**
ils	**ont dit**	ils	**dissent**

CONSTRUCTIONS

dire qch à qn   to tell sb sth
dire à qn de faire qch   to tell sb to do sth
cela ne me dit rien   I don't fancy it
on dirait du poulet   it tastes like chicken
on dirait Jean   it looks like John

36 donner
to give

also **accepter**
to accept

PRESENT PARTICIPLE
donnant

causer
to cause

PAST PARTICIPLE
donné

laver
to wash

PRESENT		IMPERFECT	
je	donne	je	donnais
tu	donnes	tu	donnais
il	donne	il	donnait
nous	donnons	nous	donnions
vous	donnez	vous	donniez
ils	donnent	ils	donnaient

FUTURE
je	donnerai
tu	donneras
il	donnera
nous	donnerons
vous	donnerez
ils	donneront

IMPERATIVE
donne
donnons
donnez

CONDITIONAL
je	donnerais
tu	donnerais
il	donnerait
nous	donnerions
vous	donneriez
ils	donneraient

poser
to put

rêver
to dream

PAST HISTORIC		PRESENT SUBJUNCTIVE	
je	donnai	je	donne
tu	donnas	tu	donnes
il	donna	il	donne
nous	donnâmes	nous	donnions
vous	donnâtes	vous	donniez
ils	donnèrent	ils	donnent

PERFECT		PAST SUBJUNCTIVE	
j'	ai donné	je	donnasse
tu	as donné	tu	donnasses
il	a donné	il	donnât
nous	avons donné	nous	donnassions
vous	avez donné	vous	donnassiez
ils	ont donné	ils	donnassent

CONSTRUCTIONS

donner qch à qn to give sb sth
donner quelque chose à faire à qn to give sb something to do
donner à boire à qn to give sb something to drink
cela me donne soif this makes me (feel) thirsty
donner sur to open onto; to overlook

37 dormir
to sleep

also **s'endormir**
to fall asleep

PRESENT PARTICIPLE
dormant

PAST PARTICIPLE
dormi

PRESENT		IMPERFECT	
je	**dors**	je	**dormais**
tu	**dors**	tu	**dormais**
il	**dort**	il	**dormait**
nous	**dormons**	nous	**dormions**
vous	**dormez**	vous	**dormiez**
ils	**dorment**	ils	**dormaient**

		FUTURE	
		je	**dormirai**
		tu	**dormiras**
		il	**dormira**
		nous	**dormirons**
		vous	**dormirez**
		ils	**dormiront**

IMPERATIVE		CONDITIONAL	
	dors	je	**dormirais**
	dormons	tu	**dormirais**
	dormez	il	**dormirait**
		nous	**dormirions**
		vous	**dormiriez**
		ils	**dormiraient**

PAST HISTORIC		PRESENT SUBJUNCTIVE	
je	dormis	je	dorme
tu	dormis	tu	dormes
il	dormit	il	dorme
nous	dormîmes	nous	dormions
vous	dormîtes	vous	dormiez
ils	dormirent	ils	dorment

PERFECT		PAST SUBJUNCTIVE	
j'	ai dormi	je	dormisse
tu	as dormi	tu	dormisses
il	a dormi	il	dormît
nous	avons dormi	nous	dormissions
vous	avez dormi	vous	dormissiez
ils	ont dormi	ils	dormissent

CONSTRUCTIONS

il dort he's asleep
j'ai mal dormi I didn't sleep well
il dort d'un sommeil léger he's a light sleeper
je n'ai pas dormi de la nuit I didn't sleep a wink (all night)

38 écrire
to write

also **décrire**
  to describe

PRESENT PARTICIPLE
écrivant

inscrire
  to write

PAST PARTICIPLE
écrit

souscrire
  to subscribe

PRESENT		IMPERFECT	
j'	écris	j'	écrivais
tu	écris	tu	écrivais
il	écrit	il	écrivait
nous	écrivons	nous	écrivions
vous	écrivez	vous	écriviez
ils	écrivent	ils	écrivaient

FUTURE
j'	écrirai
tu	écriras
il	écrira
nous	écrirons
vous	écrirez
ils	écriront

IMPERATIVE
écris
écrivons
écrivez

CONDITIONAL
j'	écrirais
tu	écrirais
il	écrirait
nous	écririons
vous	écririez
ils	écriraient

to write

transcrire
to transcribe

PAST HISTORIC		PRESENT SUBJUNCTIVE	
j'	écrivis	j'	écrive
tu	écrivis	tu	écrives
il	écrivit	il	écrive
nous	écrivîmes	nous	écrivions
vous	écrivîtes	vous	écriviez
ils	écrivirent	ils	écrivent

PERFECT		PAST SUBJUNCTIVE	
j'	ai écrit	j'	écrivisse
tu	as écrit	tu	écrivisses
il	a écrit	il	écrivît
nous	avons écrit	nous	écrivissions
vous	avez écrit	vous	écrivissiez
ils	ont écrit	ils	écrivissent

CONSTRUCTIONS
écrit à la main/à la machine   handwritten/typed
appeler s'écrit avec deux p   appeler is written with
two ps

39 entrer
to enter

PRESENT PARTICIPLE
entrant

PAST PARTICIPLE
entré

PRESENT		IMPERFECT	
j'	entre	j'	entrais
tu	entres	tu	entrais
il	entre	il	entrait
nous	entrons	nous	entrions
vous	entrez	vous	entriez
ils	entrent	ils	entraient

		FUTURE	
		j'	entrerai
		tu	entreras
		il	entrera
		nous	entrerons
		vous	entrerez
		ils	entreront

IMPERATIVE		CONDITIONAL	
	entre	j'	entrerais
	entrons	tu	entrerais
	entrez	il	entrerait
		nous	entrerions
		vous	entreriez
		ils	entreraient

PAST HISTORIC		PRESENT SUBJUNCTIVE	
j'	entrai	j'	entre
tu	entras	tu	entres
il	entra	il	entre
nous	entrâmes	nous	entrions
vous	entrâtes	vous	entriez
ils	entrèrent	ils	entrent
PERFECT		PAST SUBJUNCTIVE	
je	suis entré	j'	entrasse
tu	es entré	tu	entrasses
il	est entré	il	entrât
nous	sommes entrés	nous	entrassions
vous	êtes entré(s)	vous	entrassiez
ils	sont entrés	ils	entrassent

CONSTRUCTIONS

entrer dans une pièce/une voiture   to go (*or* come) into a
room/get into a car
faire entrer qn   to show *or* ask sb in
entrer dans un club/une firme   to join a club/firm
ça n'entre pas dans ce tiroir   it won't go into this drawer

40 envoyer
to send

also **renvoyer**
to send back

PRESENT PARTICIPLE
envoyant

PAST PARTICIPLE
envoyé

PRESENT		IMPERFECT	
j'	envoie	j'	envoyais
tu	envoies	tu	envoyais
il	envoie	il	envoyait
nous	envoyons	nous	envoyions
vous	envoyez	vous	envoyiez
ils	envoient	ils	envoyaient

		FUTURE	
		j'	enverrai
		tu	enverras
		il	enverra
		nous	enverrons
		vous	enverrez
		ils	enverront

IMPERATIVE		CONDITIONAL	
	envoie	j'	enverrais
	envoyons	tu	enverrais
	envoyez	il	enverrait
		nous	enverrions
		vous	enverriez
		ils	enverraient

PAST HISTORIC		PRESENT SUBJUNCTIVE	
j'	envoyai	j'	envoie
tu	envoyas	tu	envoies
il	envoya	il	envoie
nous	envoyâmes	nous	envoyions
vous	envoyâtes	vous	envoyiez
ils	envoyèrent	ils	envoient

PERFECT		PAST SUBJUNCTIVE	
j'	ai envoyé	j'	envoyasse
tu	as envoyé	tu	envoyasses
il	a envoyé	il	envoyât
nous	avons envoyé	nous	envoyassions
vous	avez envoyé	vous	envoyassiez
ils	ont envoyé	ils	envoyassent

CONSTRUCTIONS
envoyer chercher qn/qch   to send for sb/sth

41 espérer
to hope

also **accélérer**
to accelerate

PRESENT PARTICIPLE
espérant

céder
to give up

PAST PARTICIPLE
espéré

compléter
to complete

PRESENT		IMPERFECT	
j'	espère	j'	espérais
tu	espères	tu	espérais
il	espère	il	espérait
nous	espérons	nous	espérions
vous	espérez	vous	espériez
ils	espèrent	ils	espéraient

		FUTURE	
		j'	espérerai
		tu	espéreras
		il	espérera
		nous	espérerons
		vous	espérerez
		ils	espéreront

IMPERATIVE		CONDITIONAL	
	espère	j'	espérerais
	espérons	tu	espérerais
	espérez	il	espérerait
		nous	espérerions
		vous	espéreriez
		ils	espéreraient

régler
to settle

sécher
to dry

PAST HISTORIC		PRESENT SUBJUNCTIVE	
j'	espérai	j'	espère
tu	espéras	tu	espères
il	espéra	il	espère
nous	espérâmes	nous	espérions
vous	espérâtes	vous	espériez
ils	espérèrent	ils	espèrent

PERFECT		PAST SUBJUNCTIVE	
j'	ai espéré	j'	espérasse
tu	as espéré	tu	espérasses
il	a espéré	il	espérât
nous	avons espéré	nous	espérassions
vous	avez espéré	vous	espérassiez
ils	ont espéré	ils	espérassent

CONSTRUCTIONS

espérer faire qch   to hope to do sth
viendra-t-il? – je l'espère (bien)   will he come? – I
(certainly) hope so
j'espère bien n'avoir rien oublié   I hope I haven't
forgotten anything

42 être
to be

PRESENT PARTICIPLE
étant

PAST PARTICIPLE
été

PRESENT		IMPERFECT	
je	**suis**	j'	**étais**
tu	**es**	tu	**étais**
il	**est**	il	**était**
nous	**sommes**	nous	**étions**
vous	**êtes**	vous	**étiez**
ils	**sont**	ils	**étaient**

		FUTURE	
		je	**serai**
		tu	**seras**
		il	**sera**
		nous	**serons**
		vous	**serez**
		ils	**seront**

IMPERATIVE		CONDITIONAL	
	sois	je	**serais**
	soyons	tu	**serais**
	soyez	il	**serait**
		nous	**serions**
		vous	**seriez**
		ils	**seraient**

PAST HISTORIC		PRESENT SUBJUNCTIVE	
je	fus	je	sois
tu	fus	tu	sois
il	fut	il	soit
nous	fûmes	nous	soyons
vous	fûtes	vous	soyez
ils	furent	ils	soient

PERFECT		PAST SUBJUNCTIVE	
j'	ai été	je	fusse
tu	as été	tu	fusses
il	a été	il	fût
nous	avons été	nous	fussions
vous	avez été	vous	fussiez
ils	ont été	ils	fussent

CONSTRUCTIONS

il est peintre he's a painter
quel jour sommes-nous? – nous sommes le 12 mars
what's today's date? – it's March 12th
à qui est ce cahier? – il est à elle whose jotter is this? –
it's hers

43 faire

to do; to make   *also* **contrefaire**
                         to forge

PRESENT PARTICIPLE
faisant

défaire
    to undo

PAST PARTICIPLE
fait

refaire
    to redo

PRESENT		IMPERFECT	
je	fais	je	faisais
tu	fais	tu	faisais
il	fait	il	faisait
nous	faisons	nous	faisions
vous	faites	vous	faisiez
ils	font	ils	faisaient

FUTURE
je	ferai
tu	feras
il	fera
nous	ferons
vous	ferez
ils	feront

IMPERATIVE	CONDITIONAL	
fais	je	ferais
faisons	tu	ferais
faites	il	ferait
	nous	ferions
	vous	feriez
	ils	feraient

satisfaire
to satisfy

PAST HISTORIC		PRESENT SUBJUNCTIVE	
je	fis	je	fasse
tu	fis	tu	fasses
il	fit	il	fasse
nous	fîmes	nous	fassions
vous	fîtes	vous	fassiez
ils	firent	ils	fassent
PERFECT		PAST SUBJUNCTIVE	
j'	ai fait	je	fisse
tu	as fait	tu	fisses
il	a fait	il	fît
nous	avons fait	nous	fissions
vous	avez fait	vous	fissiez
ils	ont fait	ils	fissent

CONSTRUCTIONS
faire la vaisselle/la cuisine to do the dishes/the cooking
faire une promenade/des courses to go for a
walk/go shopping
il fait beau/du vent it's nice/windy
faire faire qch to have sth done *or* made

44 falloir
to be necessary

PRESENT PARTICIPLE
not used

PAST PARTICIPLE
fallu

PRESENT **il faut**	IMPERFECT **il fallait**
	FUTURE **il faudra**
IMPERATIVE *not used*	CONDITIONAL **il faudrait**

to be necessary

PAST HISTORIC **il fallut**	PRESENT SUBJUNCTIVE **il faille**
PERFECT **il a fallu**	PAST SUBJUNCTIVE **il fallût**

CONSTRUCTIONS

il lui faut quelqu'un pour l'aider   he needs somebody to help him

il faut qu'il parte   he'll have to *or* has to go

il faut être prudent   you have to be careful

45 finir
to finish

also **agir**
to act

PRESENT PARTICIPLE
finissant

bâtir
to build

PAST PARTICIPLE
fini

durcir
to harden

PRESENT		IMPERFECT	
je	finis	je	finissais
tu	finis	tu	finissais
il	finit	il	finissait
nous	finissons	nous	finissions
vous	finissez	vous	finissiez
ils	finissent	ils	finissaient

		FUTURE	
		je	finirai
		tu	finiras
		il	finira
		nous	finirons
		vous	finirez
		ils	finiront

IMPERATIVE	CONDITIONAL	
finis	je	finirais
finissons	tu	finirais
finissez	il	finirait
	nous	finirions
	vous	finiriez
	ils	finiraient

guérir
  to heal

réunir
  to reunite

PAST HISTORIC		PRESENT SUBJUNCTIVE	
je	finis	je	finisse
tu	finis	tu	finisses
il	finit	il	finisse
nous	finîmes	nous	finissions
vous	finîtes	vous	finissiez
ils	finirent	ils	finissent

PERFECT		PAST SUBJUNCTIVE	
j'	ai fini	je	finisse
tu	as fini	tu	finisses
il	a fini	il	finît
nous	avons fini	nous	finissions
vous	avez fini	vous	finissiez
ils	ont fini	ils	finissent

CONSTRUCTIONS

finir de faire qch   to finish doing sth
il a fini par comprendre   he finally understood
tout finira par s'arranger   everything will work out in the
end
le film finit bien   the film has a happy ending

46 fuir
to flee

also **s'enfuir**
to run away

PRESENT PARTICIPLE
fuyant

PAST PARTICIPLE
fui

PRESENT		IMPERFECT	
je	**fuis**	je	**fuyais**
tu	**fuis**	tu	**fuyais**
il	**fuit**	il	**fuyait**
nous	**fuyons**	nous	**fuyions**
vous	**fuyez**	vous	**fuyiez**
ils	**fuient**	ils	**fuyaient**

		FUTURE	
		je	**fuirai**
		tu	**fuiras**
		il	**fuira**
		nous	**fuirons**
		vous	**fuirez**
		ils	**fuiront**

IMPERATIVE		CONDITIONAL	
	fuis	je	**fuirais**
	fuyons	tu	**fuirais**
	fuyez	il	**fuirait**
		nous	**fuirions**
		vous	**fuiriez**
		ils	**fuiraient**

PAST HISTORIC		PRESENT SUBJUNCTIVE	
je	fuis	je	fuie
tu	fuis	tu	fuies
il	fuit	il	fuie
nous	fuîmes	nous	fuyions
vous	fuîtes	vous	fuyiez
ils	fuirent	ils	fuient
PERFECT		PAST SUBJUNCTIVE	
j'	ai fui	je	fuisse
tu	as fui	tu	fuisses
il	a fui	il	fuît
nous	avons fui	nous	fuissions
vous	avez fui	vous	fuissiez
ils	ont fui	ils	fuissent

CONSTRUCTIONS

fuir devant un danger/ses responsabilités to run away
from danger/one's responsibilities

47 haïr
to hate

PRESENT PARTICIPLE
haïssant

PAST PARTICIPLE
haï

PRESENT		IMPERFECT	
je	hais	je	haïssais
tu	hais	tu	haïssais
il	hait	il	haïssait
nous	haïssons	nous	haïssions
vous	haïssez	vous	haïssiez
ils	haïssent	ils	haïssaient

		FUTURE	
		je	haïrai
		tu	haïras
		il	haïra
		nous	haïrons
		vous	haïrez
		ils	haïront

IMPERATIVE		CONDITIONAL	
	hais	je	haïrais
	haïssons	tu	haïrais
	haïssez	il	haïrait
		nous	haïrions
		vous	haïriez
		ils	haïraient

PAST HISTORIC	PRESENT SUBJUNCTIVE
je haïs	je haïsse
tu haïs	tu haïsses
il haït	il haïsse
nous haïmes	nous haïssions
vous haïtes	vous haïssiez
ils haïrent	ils haïssent

PERFECT	PAST SUBJUNCTIVE
j' ai haï	je haïsse
tu as haï	tu haïsses
il a haï	il haït
nous avons haï	nous haïssions
vous avez haï	vous haïssiez
ils ont haï	ils haïssent

48 interdire
to forbid

also **contredire**
to contradict

PRESENT PARTICIPLE
interdisant

prédire
to predict

PAST PARTICIPLE
interdit

PRESENT		IMPERFECT	
j'	interdis	j'	interdisais
tu	interdis	tu	interdisais
il	interdit	il	interdisait
nous	interdisons	nous	interdisions
vous	interdisez	vous	interdisiez
ils	interdisent	ils	interdisaient

		FUTURE	
		j'	interdirai
		tu	interdiras
		il	interdira
		nous	interdirons
		vous	interdirez
		ils	interdiront

IMPERATIVE		CONDITIONAL	
	interdis	j'	interdirais
	interdisons	tu	interdirais
	interdisez	il	interdirait
		nous	interdirions
		vous	interdiriez
		ils	interdiraient

PAST HISTORIC		PRESENT SUBJUNCTIVE	
j'	interdis	j'	interdise
tu	interdis	tu	interdises
il	interdit	il	interdise
nous	interdîmes	nous	interdisions
vous	interdîtes	vous	interdisiez
ils	interdirent	ils	interdisent

PERFECT		PAST SUBJUNCTIVE	
j'	ai interdit	j'	interdisse
tu	as interdit	tu	interdisses
il	a interdit	il	interdît
nous	avons interdit	nous	interdissions
vous	avez interdit	vous	interdissiez
ils	ont interdit	ils	interdissent

CONSTRUCTIONS
interdire à qn de faire qch   to forbid sb to do sth
il m'a interdit l'alcool/le tabac   he's forbidden me to
drink/smoke
il est interdit de fumer   smoking is prohibited
stationnement interdit   no parking

49 introduire
to introduce

PRESENT PARTICIPLE
introduisant

PAST PARTICIPLE
introduit

PRESENT		IMPERFECT	
j'	introduis	j'	introduisais
tu	introduis	tu	introduisais
il	introduit	il	introduisait
nous	introduisons	nous	introduisions
vous	introduisez	vous	introduisiez
ils	introduisent	ils	introduisaient

		FUTURE	
		j'	introduirai
		tu	introduiras
		il	introduira
		nous	introduirons
		vous	introduirez
		ils	introduiront

IMPERATIVE		CONDITIONAL	
	introduis	j'	introduirais
	introduisons	tu	introduirais
	introduisez	il	introduirait
		nous	introduirions
		vous	introduiriez
		ils	introduiraient

PAST HISTORIC		PRESENT SUBJUNCTIVE	
j'	introduisis	j'	introduise
tu	introduisis	tu	introduises
il	introduisit	il	introduise
nous	introduisîmes	nous	introduisions
vous	introduisîtes	vous	introduisiez
ils	introduisirent	ils	introduisent

PERFECT		PAST SUBJUNCTIVE	
j'	ai introduit	j'	introduisisse
tu	as introduit	tu	introduisisses
il	a introduit	il	introduisît
nous	avons introduit	nous	introduisissions
vous	avez introduit	vous	introduisissiez
ils	ont introduit	ils	introduisissent

CONSTRUCTIONS

il a introduit sa clef dans la serrure he inserted his key in the lock

il m'a introduit dans le salon he showed me into the lounge

s'introduire dans une pièce to get into a room

50 jeter
to throw

also **breveter**
to patent

PRESENT PARTICIPLE
jetant

étiqueter
to label

PAST PARTICIPLE
jeté

feuilleter
to leaf through

PRESENT		IMPERFECT	
je	jette	je	jetais
tu	jettes	tu	jetais
il	jette	il	jetait
nous	jetons	nous	jetions
vous	jetez	vous	jetiez
ils	jettent	ils	jetaient

		FUTURE	
		je	jetterai
		tu	jetteras
		il	jettera
		nous	jetterons
		vous	jetterez
		ils	jetteront

IMPERATIVE		CONDITIONAL	
	jette	je	jetterais
	jetons	tu	jetterais
	jetez	il	jetterait
		nous	jetterions
		vous	jetteriez
		ils	jetteraient

projeter
to plan

rejeter
to reject

PAST HISTORIC		PRESENT SUBJUNCTIVE	
je	jetai	je	jette
tu	jetas	tu	jettes
il	jeta	il	jette
nous	jetâmes	nous	jetions
vous	jetâtes	vous	jetiez
ils	jetèrent	ils	jettent
PERFECT		PAST SUBJUNCTIVE	
j'	ai jeté	je	jetasse
tu	as jeté	tu	jetasses
il	a jeté	il	jetât
nous	avons jeté	nous	jetassions
vous	avez jeté	vous	jetassiez
ils	ont jeté	ils	jetassent

CONSTRUCTIONS

jeter qch à qn   to throw sth to sb; to throw sth at sb
jeter qch par terre/par la fenêtre   to throw sth down/out of the window
jeter qn dehors *or* **à la porte**   to throw sb out

51 joindre
to join

also **adjoindre**
to attach

PRESENT PARTICIPLE
joignant

rejoindre
to rejoin

PAST PARTICIPLE
joint

PRESENT		IMPERFECT	
je	joins	je	joignais
tu	joins	tu	joignais
il	joint	il	joignait
nous	joignons	nous	joignions
vous	joignez	vous	joigniez
ils	joignent	ils	joignaient

		FUTURE	
		je	joindrai
		tu	joindras
		il	joindra
		nous	joindrons
		vous	joindrez
		ils	joindront

IMPERATIVE		CONDITIONAL	
	joins	je	joindrais
	joignons	tu	joindrais
	joignez	il	joindrait
		nous	joindrions
		vous	joindriez
		ils	joindraient

PAST HISTORIC		PRESENT SUBJUNCTIVE	
je	joignis	je	joigne
tu	joignis	tu	joignes
il	joignit	il	joigne
nous	joignîmes	nous	joignions
vous	joignîtes	vous	joigniez
ils	joignirent	ils	joignent

PERFECT		PAST SUBJUNCTIVE	
j'	ai joint	je	joignisse
tu	as joint	tu	joignisses
il	a joint	il	joignît
nous	avons joint	nous	joignissions
vous	avez joint	vous	joignissiez
ils	ont joint	ils	joignissent

CONSTRUCTIONS

joindre les mains to clasp one's hands (together)
voir la lettre ci-jointe see the enclosed letter
elle joint l'intelligence à la beauté she combines
intelligence and beauty
se joindre à to join

52 lever
to lift

also **amener**
to bring

PRESENT PARTICIPLE
levant

élever
to raise

PAST PARTICIPLE
levé

enlever
to remove

PRESENT		IMPERFECT	
je	lève	je	levais
tu	lèves	tu	levais
il	lève	il	levait
nous	levons	nous	levions
vous	levez	vous	leviez
ils	lèvent	ils	levaient

		FUTURE	
		je	lèverai
		tu	lèveras
		il	lèvera
		nous	lèverons
		vous	lèverez
		ils	lèveront

IMPERATIVE		CONDITIONAL	
lève		je	lèverais
levons		tu	lèverais
levez		il	lèverait
		nous	lèverions
		vous	lèveriez
		ils	lèveraient

mener
to lead

peser
to weigh

PAST HISTORIC		PRESENT SUBJUNCTIVE	
je	levai	je	lève
tu	levas	tu	lèves
il	leva	il	lève
nous	levâmes	nous	levions
vous	levâtes	vous	leviez
ils	levèrent	ils	lèvent

PERFECT		PAST SUBJUNCTIVE	
j'	ai levé	je	levasse
tu	as levé	tu	levasses
il	a levé	il	levât
nous	avons levé	nous	levassions
vous	avez levé	vous	levassiez
ils	ont levé	ils	levassent

CONSTRUCTIONS
lever les yeux   to look up
levez la main!   put your hand up!
lever son verre à qn   to raise one's glass to sb
se lever   to get up; to rise
le jour/la brume se lève   day breaks/the mist is clearing

117

53 lire
to read   *also* **élire**
            to elect

PRESENT PARTICIPLE
lisant

PAST PARTICIPLE
lu

PRESENT		IMPERFECT	
je	lis	je	lisais
tu	lis	tu	lisais
il	lit	il	lisait
nous	lisons	nous	lisions
vous	lisez	vous	lisiez
ils	lisent	ils	lisaient

		FUTURE	
		je	lirai
		tu	liras
		il	lira
		nous	lirons
		vous	lirez
		ils	liront

IMPERATIVE		CONDITIONAL	
	lis	je	lirais
	lisons	tu	lirais
	lisez	il	lirait
		nous	lirions
		vous	liriez
		ils	liraient

PAST HISTORIC		PRESENT SUBJUNCTIVE	
je	lus	je	lise
tu	lus	tu	lises
il	lut	il	lise
nous	lûmes	nous	lisions
vous	lûtes	vous	lisiez
ils	lurent	ils	lisent

PERFECT		PAST SUBJUNCTIVE	
j'	ai lu	je	lusse
tu	as lu	tu	lusses
il	a lu	il	lût
nous	avons lu	nous	lussions
vous	avez lu	vous	lussiez
ils	ont lu	ils	lussent

CONSTRUCTIONS

je lui ai lu une histoire   I read him a story
c'est un livre à lire   it's a book you should read

54 manger
to eat

also **arranger**
to arrange

PRESENT PARTICIPLE
mangeant

bouger
to move

PAST PARTICIPLE
mangé

dégager
to clear

PRESENT		IMPERFECT	
je	mange	je	mangeais
tu	manges	tu	mangeais
il	mange	il	mangeait
nous	mangeons	nous	mangions
vous	mangez	vous	mangiez
ils	mangent	ils	mangeaient

		FUTURE	
		je	mangerai
		tu	mangeras
		il	mangera
		nous	mangerons
		vous	mangerez
		ils	mangeront

IMPERATIVE		CONDITIONAL	
	mange	je	mangerais
	mangeons	tu	mangerais
	mangez	il	mangerait
		nous	mangerions
		vous	mangeriez
		ils	mangeraient

diriger
to manage

loger
to accommodate

PAST HISTORIC		PRESENT SUBJUNCTIVE	
je	mangeai	je	mange
tu	mangeas	tu	manges
il	mangea	il	mange
nous	mangeâmes	nous	mangions
vous	mangeâtes	vous	mangiez
ils	mangèrent	ils	mangent
PERFECT		PAST SUBJUNCTIVE	
j'	ai mangé	je	mangeasse
tu	as mangé	tu	mangeasses
il	a mangé	il	mangeât
nous	avons mangé	nous	mangeassions
vous	avez mangé	vous	mangeassiez
ils	ont mangé	ils	mangeassent

CONSTRUCTIONS
manger comme quatre   to eat like a horse
est-ce que ça se mange?   is it edible?

55 maudire
to curse

PRESENT PARTICIPLE
maudissant

PAST PARTICIPLE
maudit

PRESENT		IMPERFECT	
je	maudis	je	maudissais
tu	maudis	tu	maudissais
il	maudit	il	maudissait
nous	maudissons	nous	maudissions
vous	maudissez	vous	maudissiez
ils	maudissent	ils	maudissaient

		FUTURE	
		je	maudirai
		tu	maudiras
		il	maudira
		nous	maudirons
		vous	maudirez
		ils	maudiront

IMPERATIVE		CONDITIONAL	
	maudis	je	maudirais
	maudissons	tu	maudirais
	maudissez	il	maudirait
		nous	maudirions
		vous	maudiriez
		ils	maudiraient

PAST HISTORIC		PRESENT SUBJUNCTIVE	
je	maudis	je	maudisse
tu	maudis	tu	maudisses
il	maudit	il	maudisse
nous	maudîmes	nous	maudissions
vous	maudîtes	vous	maudissiez
ils	maudirent	ils	maudissent

PERFECT		PAST SUBJUNCTIVE	
j'	ai maudit	je	maudisse
tu	as maudit	tu	maudisses
il	a maudit	il	maudît
nous	avons maudit	nous	maudissions
vous	avez maudit	vous	maudissiez
ils	ont maudit	ils	maudissent

CONSTRUCTIONS

ce maudit stylo ne marche pas!　this blasted pen won't work!

123

56 mettre
to put

also **admettre**
to admit

PRESENT PARTICIPLE
mettant

commettre
to commit

PAST PARTICIPLE
mis

émettre
to emit

PRESENT		IMPERFECT	
je	**mets**	je	**mettais**
tu	**mets**	tu	**mettais**
il	**met**	il	**mettait**
nous	**mettons**	nous	**mettions**
vous	**mettez**	vous	**mettiez**
ils	**mettent**	ils	**mettaient**

		FUTURE	
		je	**mettrai**
		tu	**mettras**
		il	**mettra**
		nous	**mettrons**
		vous	**mettrez**
		ils	**mettront**

IMPERATIVE		CONDITIONAL	
	mets	je	**mettrais**
	mettons	tu	**mettrais**
	mettez	il	**mettrait**
		nous	**mettrions**
		vous	**mettriez**
		ils	**mettraient**

soumettre
to submit

transmettre
to transmit

PAST HISTORIC		PRESENT SUBJUNCTIVE	
je	mis	je	mette
tu	mis	tu	mettes
il	mit	il	mette
nous	mîmes	nous	mettions
vous	mîtes	vous	mettiez
ils	mirent	ils	mettent

PERFECT		PAST SUBJUNCTIVE	
j'	ai mis	je	misse
tu	as mis	tu	misses
il	a mis	il	mît
nous	avons mis	nous	missions
vous	avez mis	vous	missiez
ils	ont mis	ils	missent

CONSTRUCTIONS
j'ai mis 2 heures à le faire I took 2 hours to do it
elle n'a rien à se mettre she's nothing to wear
se mettre à faire qch to start doing sth
se mettre au travail to set to work

57 monter

to go up

PRESENT PARTICIPLE
montant

PAST PARTICIPLE
monté

PRESENT		IMPERFECT	
je	monte	je	montais
tu	montes	tu	montais
il	monte	il	montait
nous	montons	nous	montions
vous	montez	vous	montiez
ils	montent	ils	montaient

		FUTURE	
		je	monterai
		tu	monteras
		il	montera
		nous	monterons
		vous	monterez
		ils	monteront

IMPERATIVE		CONDITIONAL	
	monte	je	monterais
	montons	tu	monterais
	montez	il	monterait
		nous	monterions
		vous	monteriez
		ils	monteraient

PAST HISTORIC	PRESENT SUBJUNCTIVE
je montai	je monte
tu montas	tu montes
il monta	il monte
nous montâmes	nous montions
vous montâtes	vous montiez
ils montèrent	ils montent

PERFECT	PAST SUBJUNCTIVE
je suis monté	je montasse
tu es monté	tu montasses
il est monté	il montât
nous sommes montés	nous montassions
vous êtes monté(s)	vous montassiez
ils sont montés	ils montassent

CONSTRUCTIONS

monter dans un train/un avion to get on a train/plane
monter en voiture to get into a car
monter à bicyclette/cheval to get on a bicycle/horse; to ride a bicycle/horse
il a monté la valise he took the case up

58 mordre
to bite

also **tordre**
to twist

PRESENT PARTICIPLE
mordant

PAST PARTICIPLE
mordu

PRESENT		IMPERFECT	
je	**mords**	je	**mordais**
tu	**mords**	tu	**mordais**
il	**mord**	il	**mordait**
nous	**mordons**	nous	**mordions**
vous	**mordez**	vous	**mordiez**
ils	**mordent**	ils	**mordaient**

FUTURE
je	**mordrai**
tu	**mordras**
il	**mordra**
nous	**mordrons**
vous	**mordrez**
ils	**mordront**

IMPERATIVE

mords
mordons
mordez

CONDITIONAL
je	**mordrais**
tu	**mordrais**
il	**mordrait**
nous	**mordrions**
vous	**mordriez**
ils	**mordraient**

PAST HISTORIC		PRESENT SUBJUNCTIVE	
je	mordis	je	morde
tu	mordis	tu	mordes
il	mordit	il	morde
nous	mordîmes	nous	mordions
vous	mordîtes	vous	mordiez
ils	mordirent	ils	mordent

PERFECT		PAST SUBJUNCTIVE	
j'	ai mordu	je	mordisse
tu	as mordu	tu	mordisses
il	a mordu	il	mordît
nous	avons mordu	nous	mordissions
vous	avez mordu	vous	mordissiez
ils	ont mordu	ils	mordissent

CONSTRUCTIONS

mordre qn à la main   to bite sb's hand
mordre dans une pomme   to bite into an apple
mordu de football   mad keen on football
mordre à l'hameçon   to rise to the bait

59 moudre
to grind

PRESENT PARTICIPLE
moulant

PAST PARTICIPLE
moulu

PRESENT		IMPERFECT	
je	**mouds**	je	**moulais**
tu	**mouds**	tu	**moulais**
il	**moud**	il	**moulait**
nous	**moulons**	nous	**moulions**
vous	**moulez**	vous	**mouliez**
ils	**moulent**	ils	**moulaient**

FUTURE	
je	**moudrai**
tu	**moudras**
il	**moudra**
nous	**moudrons**
vous	**moudrez**
ils	**moudront**

IMPERATIVE
mouds
moulons
moulez

CONDITIONAL	
je	**moudrais**
tu	**moudrais**
il	**moudrait**
nous	**moudrions**
vous	**moudriez**
ils	**moudraient**

PAST HISTORIC		PRESENT SUBJUNCTIVE	
je	moulus	je	moule
tu	moulus	tu	moules
il	moulut	il	moule
nous	moulûmes	nous	moulions
vous	moulûtes	vous	mouliez
ils	moulurent	ils	moulent

PERFECT		PAST SUBJUNCTIVE	
j'	ai moulu	je	moulusse
tu	as moulu	tu	moulusses
il	a moulu	il	moulût
nous	avons moulu	nous	moulussions
vous	avez moulu	vous	moulussiez
ils	ont moulu	ils	moulussent

CONSTRUCTIONS

je l'aimerais moulu très fin, s'il vous plaît I'd like it very finely ground, please

60 mourir
to die

PRESENT PARTICIPLE
mourant

PAST PARTICIPLE
mort

PRESENT		IMPERFECT	
je	meurs	je	mourais
tu	meurs	tu	mourais
il	meurt	il	mourait
nous	mourons	nous	mourions
vous	mourez	vous	mouriez
ils	meurent	ils	mouraient

		FUTURE	
		je	mourrai
		tu	mourras
		il	mourra
		nous	mourrons
		vous	mourrez
		ils	mourront

IMPERATIVE	CONDITIONAL	
meurs	je	mourrais
mourons	tu	mourrais
mourez	il	mourrait
	nous	mourrions
	vous	mourriez
	ils	mourraient

PAST HISTORIC	PRESENT SUBJUNCTIVE
je **mourus**	je **meure**
tu **mourus**	tu **meures**
il **mourut**	il **meure**
nous **mourûmes**	nous **mourions**
vous **mourûtes**	vous **mouriez**
ils **moururent**	ils **meurent**

PERFECT	PAST SUBJUNCTIVE
je **suis mort**	je **mourusse**
tu **es mort**	tu **mourusses**
il **est mort**	il **mourût**
nous **sommes morts**	nous **mourussions**
vous **êtes mort(s)**	vous **mourussiez**
ils **sont morts**	ils **mourussent**

CONSTRUCTIONS
il est mort he's dead
il est mort en 1960 he died in 1960
mourir de faim/froid to die of hunger/cold
être mort de peur to be scared to death
mourir d'envie de faire qch to be dying to do sth

61 mouvoir
to move

PRESENT PARTICIPLE
mouvant

PAST PARTICIPLE
mû (*NB*: **mue, mus, mues**)

PRESENT		IMPERFECT	
je	**meus**	je	**mouvais**
tu	**meus**	tu	**mouvais**
il	**meut**	il	**mouvait**
nous	**mouvons**	nous	**mouvions**
vous	**mouvez**	vous	**mouviez**
ils	**meuvent**	ils	**mouvaient**

		FUTURE	
		je	**mouvrai**
		tu	**mouvras**
		il	**mouvra**
		nous	**mouvrons**
		vous	**mouvrez**
		ils	**mouvront**

IMPERATIVE			
	meus		
	mouvons		
	mouvez		

		CONDITIONAL	
		je	**mouvrais**
		tu	**mouvrais**
		il	**mouvrait**
		nous	**mouvrions**
		vous	**mouvriez**
		ils	**mouvraient**

PAST HISTORIC		PRESENT SUBJUNCTIVE	
je	mus	je	meuve
tu	mus	tu	meuves
il	mut	il	meuve
nous	mûmes	nous	mouvions
vous	mûtes	vous	mouviez
ils	murent	ils	meuvent

PERFECT		PAST SUBJUNCTIVE	
j'	ai mû	je	musse
tu	as mû	tu	musses
il	a mû	il	mût
nous	avons mû	nous	mussions
vous	avez mû	vous	mussiez
ils	ont mû	ils	mussent

CONSTRUCTIONS

il a de la peine à se mouvoir   he has difficulty in moving

135

62 naître
to be born

PRESENT PARTICIPLE
naissant

PAST PARTICIPLE
né

PRESENT		IMPERFECT	
je	nais	je	naissais
tu	nais	tu	naissais
il	naît	il	naissait
nous	naissons	nous	naissions
vous	naissez	vous	naissiez
ils	naissent	ils	naissaient

		FUTURE	
		je	naîtrai
		tu	naîtras
		il	naîtra
		nous	naîtrons
		vous	naîtrez
		ils	naîtront

IMPERATIVE	CONDITIONAL	
nais	je	naîtrais
naissons	tu	naîtrais
naissez	il	naîtrait
	nous	naîtrions
	vous	naîtriez
	ils	naîtraient

PAST HISTORIC		PRESENT SUBJUNCTIVE	
je	naquis	je	naisse
tu	naquis	tu	naisses
il	naquit	il	naisse
nous	naquîmes	nous	naissions
vous	naquîtes	vous	naissiez
ils	naquirent	ils	naissent

PERFECT		PAST SUBJUNCTIVE	
je	suis né	je	naquisse
tu	es né	tu	naquisses
il	est né	il	naquît
nous	sommes nés	nous	naquissions
vous	êtes né(s)	vous	naquissiez
ils	sont nés	ils	naquissent

CONSTRUCTIONS

je suis né le 5 mars I was born on 5th March
il naît plus de filles que de garçons there are more girls
born than boys
faire naître des soupçons to arouse suspicion

63 nettoyer
to clean

also **aboyer**
to bark

PRESENT PARTICIPLE
nettoyant

appuyer
to lean

PAST PARTICIPLE
nettoyé

employer
to use

PRESENT		IMPERFECT	
je	nettoie	je	nettoyais
tu	nettoies	tu	nettoyais
il	nettoie	il	nettoyait
nous	nettoyons	nous	nettoyions
vous	nettoyez	vous	nettoyiez
ils	nettoient	ils	nettoyaient

FUTURE

je	nettoierai
tu	nettoieras
il	nettoiera
nous	nettoierons
vous	nettoierez
ils	nettoieront

IMPERATIVE
nettoie
nettoyons
nettoyez

CONDITIONAL

je	nettoierais
tu	nettoierais
il	nettoierait
nous	nettoierions
vous	nettoieriez
ils	nettoieraient

ennuyer
to bore

essuyer
to wipe

PAST HISTORIC		PRESENT SUBJUNCTIVE	
je	nettoyai	je	nettoie
tu	nettoyas	tu	nettoies
il	nettoya	il	nettoie
nous	nettoyâmes	nous	nettoyions
vous	nettoyâtes	vous	nettoyiez
ils	nettoyèrent	ils	nettoient

PERFECT		PAST SUBJUNCTIVE	
j'	ai nettoyé	je	nettoyasse
tu	as nettoyé	tu	nettoyasses
il	a nettoyé	il	nettoyât
nous	avons nettoyé	nous	nettoyassions
vous	avez nettoyé	vous	nettoyassiez
ils	ont nettoyé	ils	nettoyassent

CONSTRUCTIONS
nettoyer à sec   to dry-clean

64 obtenir
to get

PRESENT PARTICIPLE
obtenant

PAST PARTICIPLE
obtenu

PRESENT		IMPERFECT	
j'	obtiens	j'	obtenais
tu	obtiens	tu	obtenais
il	obtient	il	obtenait
nous	obtenons	nous	obtenions
vous	obtenez	vous	obteniez
ils	obtiennent	ils	obtenaient

		FUTURE	
		j'	obtiendrai
		tu	obtiendras
		il	obtiendra
		nous	obtiendrons
		vous	obtiendrez
		ils	obtiendront

IMPERATIVE	CONDITIONAL	
obtiens	j'	obtiendrais
obtenons	tu	obtiendrais
obtenez	il	obtiendrait
	nous	obtiendrions
	vous	obtiendriez
	ils	obtiendraient

PAST HISTORIC		PRESENT SUBJUNCTIVE	
j'	obtins	j'	obtienne
tu	obtins	tu	obtiennes
il	obtint	il	obtienne
nous	obtînmes	nous	obtenions
vous	obtîntes	vous	obteniez
ils	obtinrent	ils	obtiennent

PERFECT		PAST SUBJUNCTIVE	
j'	ai obtenu	j'	obtinsse
tu	as obtenu	tu	obtinsses
il	a obtenu	il	obtînt
nous	avons obtenu	nous	obtinssions
vous	avez obtenu	vous	obtinssiez
ils	ont obtenu	ils	obtinssent

CONSTRUCTIONS

obtenir qch de qn   to get sth from sb
obtenir de qn qu'il fasse qch   to get sb to do sth

65 offrir
to offer   *also* **souffrir**
                                       to suffer

PRESENT PARTICIPLE
offrant

PAST PARTICIPLE
offert

PRESENT		IMPERFECT	
j'	offre	j'	offrais
tu	offres	tu	offrais
il	offre	il	offrait
nous	offrons	nous	offrions
vous	offrez	vous	offriez
ils	offrent	ils	offraient

		FUTURE	
		j'	offrirai
		tu	offriras
		il	offrira
		nous	offrirons
		vous	offrirez
		ils	offriront

IMPERATIVE		CONDITIONAL	
	offre	j'	offrirais
	offrons	tu	offrirais
	offrez	il	offrirait
		nous	offririons
		vous	offririez
		ils	offriraient

142

PAST HISTORIC		PRESENT SUBJUNCTIVE	
j'	offris	j'	offre
tu	offris	tu	offres
il	offrit	il	offre
nous	offrîmes	nous	offrions
vous	offrîtes	vous	offriez
ils	offrirent	ils	offrent

PERFECT		PAST SUBJUNCTIVE	
j'	ai offert	j'	offrisse
tu	as offert	tu	offrisses
il	a offert	il	offrît
nous	avons offert	nous	offrissions
vous	avez offert	vous	offrissiez
ils	ont offert	ils	offrissent

CONSTRUCTIONS

offrir qch à qn   to give sb sth; to offer sb sth
offrir de faire qch   to offer to do sth
s'offrir un bon repas/un disque   to treat oneself to a good meal/a record
il s'est offert en otage/comme guide   he volunteered to be *or* as a hostage/guide

143

66 ouvrir
to open

also **rouvrir**
to reopen

PRESENT PARTICIPLE
ouvrant

PAST PARTICIPLE
ouvert

PRESENT		IMPERFECT	
j'	ouvre	j'	ouvrais
tu	ouvres	tu	ouvrais
il	ouvre	il	ouvrait
nous	ouvrons	nous	ouvrions
vous	ouvrez	vous	ouvriez
ils	ouvrent	ils	ouvraient

FUTURE

j'	ouvrirai
tu	ouvriras
il	ouvrira
nous	ouvrirons
vous	ouvrirez
ils	ouvriront

IMPERATIVE	CONDITIONAL	
ouvre	j'	ouvrirais
ouvrons	tu	ouvrirais
ouvrez	il	ouvrirait
	nous	ouvririons
	vous	ouvririez
	ils	ouvriraient

PAST HISTORIC		PRESENT SUBJUNCTIVE	
j'	ouvris	j'	ouvre
tu	ouvris	tu	ouvres
il	ouvrit	il	ouvre
nous	ouvrîmes	nous	ouvrions
vous	ouvrîtes	vous	ouvriez
ils	ouvrirent	ils	ouvrent

PERFECT		PAST SUBJUNCTIVE	
j'	ai ouvert	j'	ouvrisse
tu	as ouvert	tu	ouvrisses
il	a ouvert	il	ouvrît
nous	avons ouvert	nous	ouvrissions
vous	avez ouvert	vous	ouvrissiez
ils	ont ouvert	ils	ouvrissent

CONSTRUCTIONS

ouvrir une porte toute grande   to open a door wide
ouvrir l'électricité/le gaz/la radio   to switch *or* turn on the electricity/gas/radio
notre épicier ouvre le lundi   our grocer is open on Mondays
s'ouvrir   to open; to open up; to open out

145

67 paraître
to appear

also **disparaître**
to disappear

PRESENT PARTICIPLE
paraissant

PAST PARTICIPLE
paru

PRESENT		IMPERFECT	
je	parais	je	paraissais
tu	parais	tu	paraissais
il	paraît	il	paraissait
nous	paraissons	nous	paraissions
vous	paraissez	vous	paraissiez
ils	paraissent	ils	paraissaient

		FUTURE	
		je	paraîtrai
		tu	paraîtras
		il	paraîtra
		nous	paraîtrons
		vous	paraîtrez
		ils	paraîtront

IMPERATIVE		CONDITIONAL	
	parais	je	paraîtrais
	paraissons	tu	paraîtrais
	paraissez	il	paraîtrait
		nous	paraîtrions
		vous	paraîtriez
		ils	paraîtraient

PAST HISTORIC		PRESENT SUBJUNCTIVE	
je	parus	je	paraisse
tu	parus	tu	paraisses
il	parut	il	paraisse
nous	parûmes	nous	paraissions
vous	parûtes	vous	paraissiez
ils	parurent	ils	paraissent

PERFECT		PAST SUBJUNCTIVE	
j'	ai paru	je	parusse
tu	as paru	tu	parusses
il	a paru	il	parût
nous	avons paru	nous	parussions
vous	avez paru	vous	parussiez
ils	ont paru	ils	parussent

CONSTRUCTIONS

paraître faire qch   to seem to do sth
'vient de paraître'   'just out'
'à paraître prochainement'   'out soon'
il est malade, paraît-il,   il paraît qu'il est malade   he's
ill apparently

68 partir
to go, leave

PRESENT PARTICIPLE
partant

PAST PARTICIPLE
parti

PRESENT		IMPERFECT	
je	pars	je	partais
tu	pars	tu	partais
il	part	il	partait
nous	partons	nous	partions
vous	partez	vous	partiez
ils	partent	ils	partaient

		FUTURE	
		je	partirai
		tu	partiras
		il	partira
		nous	partirons
		vous	partirez
		ils	partiront

IMPERATIVE		CONDITIONAL	
	pars	je	partirais
	partons	tu	partirais
	partez	il	partirait
		nous	partirions
		vous	partiriez
		ils	partiraient

PAST HISTORIC		PRESENT SUBJUNCTIVE	
je	partis	je	parte
tu	partis	tu	partes
il	partit	il	parte
nous	partîmes	nous	partions
vous	partîtes	vous	partiez
ils	partirent	ils	partent

PERFECT		PAST SUBJUNCTIVE	
je	suis parti	je	partisse
tu	es parti	tu	partisses
il	est parti	il	partît
nous	sommes partis	nous	partissions
vous	êtes parti(s)	vous	partissiez
ils	sont partis	ils	partissent

CONSTRUCTIONS

partir en vacances/en voyage   to go (off) on holiday/on a journey
à partir du 14 juillet   as from the 14th of July
à partir de 6 F   from 6 F upwards

69 passer
to pass

also **dépasser**
to overtake

PRESENT PARTICIPLE
passant

surpasser
to surpass

PAST PARTICIPLE
passé

PRESENT		IMPERFECT	
je	passe	je	passais
tu	passes	tu	passais
il	passe	il	passait
nous	passons	nous	passions
vous	passez	vous	passiez
ils	passent	ils	passaient

		FUTURE	
		je	passerai
		tu	passeras
		il	passera
		nous	passerons
		vous	passerez
		ils	passeront

IMPERATIVE		CONDITIONAL	
	passe	je	passerais
	passons	tu	passerais
	passez	il	passerait
		nous	passerions
		vous	passeriez
		ils	passeraient

PAST HISTORIC	PRESENT SUBJUNCTIVE
je passai	je passe
tu passas	tu passes
il passa	il passe
nous passâmes	nous passions
vous passâtes	vous passiez
ils passèrent	ils passent

PERFECT	PAST SUBJUNCTIVE
j' ai passé	je passasse
tu as passé	tu passasses
il a passé	il passât
nous avons passé	nous passassions
vous avez passé	vous passassiez
ils ont passé	ils passassent

CONSTRUCTIONS

passer en courant   to run past
passer au bureau/chez un ami   to call (in) at the office/at a friend's
laisser passer qn   to let sb through *or* in *etc*
laisser passer une erreur   to overlook a mistake
passer un examen   to sit an exam

70 payer
to pay

also **balayer**
to sweep up

PRESENT PARTICIPLE
payant

débrayer
to declutch

PAST PARTICIPLE
payé

délayer
to thin down

PRESENT		IMPERFECT	
je	paye	je	payais
tu	payes	tu	payais
il	paye	il	payait
nous	payons	nous	payions
vous	payez	vous	payiez
ils	payent	ils	payaient

		FUTURE	
		je	payerai
		tu	payeras
		il	payera
		nous	payerons
		vous	payerez
		ils	payeront

IMPERATIVE		CONDITIONAL	
	paye	je	payerais
	payons	tu	payerais
	payez	il	payerait
		nous	payerions
		vous	payeriez
		ils	payeraient

effrayer
to frighten

essayer
to try

PAST HISTORIC		PRESENT SUBJUNCTIVE	
je	payai	je	paye
tu	payas	tu	payes
il	paya	il	paye
nous	payâmes	nous	payions
vous	payâtes	vous	payiez
ils	payèrent	ils	payent

PERFECT		PAST SUBJUNCTIVE	
j'	ai payé	je	payasse
tu	as payé	tu	payasses
il	a payé	il	payât
nous	avons payé	nous	payassions
vous	avez payé	vous	payassiez
ils	ont payé	ils	payassent

CONSTRUCTIONS
être payé par chèque/à l'heure   to be paid by cheque/by
the hour
est-ce qu'il t'a payé les billets?   did he pay you for the
tickets?
il l'a payé 10 F   he paid 10 F for it
il l'a payé de sa vie   it cost him his life

71 peindre
to paint

also **atteindre**
to reach

PRESENT PARTICIPLE
peignant

déteindre
to lose its colour

PAST PARTICIPLE
peint

enfreindre
to infringe

PRESENT
je	peins
tu	peins
il	peint
nous	peignons
vous	peignez
ils	peignent

IMPERFECT
je	peignais
tu	peignais
il	peignait
nous	peignions
vous	peigniez
ils	peignaient

FUTURE
je	peindrai
tu	peindras
il	peindra
nous	peindrons
vous	peindrez
ils	peindront

IMPERATIVE
peins
peignons
peignez

CONDITIONAL
je	peindrais
tu	peindrais
il	peindrait
nous	peindrions
vous	peindriez
ils	peindraient

éteindre
to put out

teindre
to dye

PAST HISTORIC		PRESENT SUBJUNCTIVE	
je	peignis	je	peigne
tu	peignis	tu	peignes
il	peignit	il	peigne
nous	peignîmes	nous	peignions
vous	peignîtes	vous	peigniez
ils	peignirent	ils	peignent

PERFECT		PAST SUBJUNCTIVE	
j'	ai peint	je	peignisse
tu	as peint	tu	peignisses
il	a peint	il	peignît
nous	avons peint	nous	peignissions
vous	avez peint	vous	peignissiez
ils	ont peint	ils	peignissent

CONSTRUCTIONS
peindre qch en bleu/à l'huile   to paint sth blue/in oils

72 perdre
to lose

PRESENT PARTICIPLE
perdant

PAST PARTICIPLE
perdu

PRESENT		IMPERFECT	
je	perds	je	perdais
tu	perds	tu	perdais
il	perd	il	perdait
nous	perdons	nous	perdions
vous	perdez	vous	perdiez
ils	perdent	ils	perdaient

		FUTURE	
		je	perdrai
		tu	perdras
		il	perdra
		nous	perdrons
		vous	perdrez
		ils	perdront

IMPERATIVE		CONDITIONAL	
	perds	je	perdrais
	perdons	tu	perdrais
	perdez	il	perdrait
		nous	perdrions
		vous	perdriez
		ils	perdraient

PAST HISTORIC		PRESENT SUBJUNCTIVE	
je	perdis	je	perde
tu	perdis	tu	perdes
il	perdit	il	perde
nous	perdîmes	nous	perdions
vous	perdîtes	vous	perdiez
ils	perdirent	ils	perdent

PERFECT		PAST SUBJUNCTIVE	
j'	ai perdu	je	perdisse
tu	as perdu	tu	perdisses
il	a perdu	il	perdît
nous	avons perdu	nous	perdissions
vous	avez perdu	vous	perdissiez
ils	ont perdu	ils	perdissent

CONSTRUCTIONS

perdre qn/qch de vue   to lose sight of sb/sth
perdre espoir/connaissance/du poids   to lose
hope/consciousness/weight
tu perds ton temps à essayer   you're wasting your time
trying
se perdre   to get lost; to disappear

73 permettre
to allow

PRESENT PARTICIPLE
permettant

PAST PARTICIPLE
permis

PRESENT		IMPERFECT	
je	**permets**	je	**permettais**
tu	**permets**	tu	**permettais**
il	**permet**	il	**permettait**
nous	**permettons**	nous	**permettions**
vous	**permettez**	vous	**permettiez**
ils	**permettent**	ils	**permettaient**

		FUTURE	
		je	**permettrai**
		tu	**permettras**
		il	**permettra**
		nous	**permettrons**
		vous	**permettrez**
		ils	**permettront**

IMPERATIVE		CONDITIONAL	
	permets	je	**permettrais**
	permettons	tu	**permettrais**
	permettez	il	**permettrait**
		nous	**permettrions**
		vous	**permettriez**
		ils	**permettraient**

PAST HISTORIC		PRESENT SUBJUNCTIVE	
je	permis	je	permette
tu	permis	tu	permettes
il	permit	il	permette
nous	permîmes	nous	permettions
vous	permîtes	vous	permettiez
ils	permirent	ils	permettent

PERFECT		PAST SUBJUNCTIVE	
j'	ai permis	je	permisse
tu	as permis	tu	permisses
il	a permis	il	permît
nous	avons permis	nous	permissions
vous	avez permis	vous	permissiez
ils	ont permis	ils	permissent

CONSTRUCTIONS

permettre à qn de faire qch   to allow sb to do sth
permettre qch à qn   to allow sb sth
mes moyens ne me le permettent pas   I can't afford it
permettez-moi de vous présenter ma sœur   may I
introduce my sister?

74 plaire
to please

also **déplaire**
to displease

PRESENT PARTICIPLE
plaisant

PAST PARTICIPLE
plu

PRESENT
je	plais
tu	plais
il	plaît
nous	plaisons
vous	plaisez
ils	plaisent

IMPERFECT
je	plaisais
tu	plaisais
il	plaisait
nous	plaisions
vous	plaisiez
ils	plaisaient

FUTURE
je	plairai
tu	plairas
il	plaira
nous	plairons
vous	plairez
ils	plairont

IMPERATIVE
plais
plaisons
plaisez

CONDITIONAL
je	plairais
tu	plairais
il	plairait
nous	plairions
vous	plairiez
ils	plairaient

PAST HISTORIC		PRESENT SUBJUNCTIVE	
je	plus	je	plaise
tu	plus	tu	plaises
il	plut	il	plaise
nous	plûmes	nous	plaisions
vous	plûtes	vous	plaisiez
ils	plurent	ils	plaisent

PERFECT		PAST SUBJUNCTIVE	
j'	ai plu	je	plusse
tu	as plu	tu	plusses
il	a plu	il	plût
nous	avons plu	nous	plussions
vous	avez plu	vous	plussiez
ils	ont plu	ils	plussent

CONSTRUCTIONS
sa maison lui plaît   she likes her house
il cherche à plaire à tout le monde   he tries to please
everybody
j'irai si ça me plaît   I'll go if I feel like it
s'il te plaît, s'il vous plaît   please
il se plaît à Paris   he likes being in Paris

75 pleuvoir
to rain

PRESENT PARTICIPLE
pleuvant

PAST PARTICIPLE
plu

PRESENT	IMPERFECT
il pleut	**il pleuvait**

FUTURE
il pleuvra

IMPERATIVE	CONDITIONAL
not used	**il pleuvrait**

PAST HISTORIC **il plut**	PRESENT SUBJUNCTIVE **il pleuve**
PERFECT **il a plu**	PAST SUBJUNCTIVE **il plût**

CONSTRUCTIONS
il pleut it's raining
il pleut à verse it's pouring

76 pourvoir
to provide

PRESENT PARTICIPLE
pourvoyant

PAST PARTICIPLE
pourvu

PRESENT		IMPERFECT	
je	**pourvois**	je	**pourvoyais**
tu	**pourvois**	tu	**pourvoyais**
il	**pourvoit**	il	**pourvoyait**
nous	**pourvoyons**	nous	**pourvoyions**
vous	**pourvoyez**	vous	**pourvoyiez**
ils	**pourvoient**	ils	**pourvoyaient**

		FUTURE	
		je	**pourvoirai**
		tu	**pourvoiras**
		il	**pourvoira**
		nous	**pourvoirons**
		vous	**pourvoirez**
		ils	**pourvoiront**

IMPERATIVE		CONDITIONAL	
	pourvois	je	**pourvoirais**
	pourvoyons	tu	**pourvoirais**
	pourvoyez	il	**pourvoirait**
		nous	**pourvoirions**
		vous	**pourvoiriez**
		ils	**pourvoiraient**

to provide

PAST HISTORIC		PRESENT SUBJUNCTIVE	
je	pourvus	je	pourvoie
tu	pourvus	tu	pourvoies
il	pourvut	il	pourvoie
nous	pourvûmes	nous	pourvoyions
vous	pourvûtes	vous	pourvoyiez
ils	pourvurent	ils	pourvoient

PERFECT		PAST SUBJUNCTIVE	
j'	ai pourvu	je	pourvusse
tu	as pourvu	tu	pourvusses
il	a pourvu	il	pourvût
nous	avons pourvu	nous	pourvussions
vous	avez pourvu	vous	pourvussiez
ils	ont pourvu	ils	pourvussent

CONSTRUCTIONS
pourvoir qch de qch to equip sth with sth
pourvoir aux besoins de qn to provide for sb's needs

77 pouvoir
to be able

PRESENT PARTICIPLE
pouvant

PAST PARTICIPLE
pu

PRESENT		IMPERFECT	
je	**peux**	je	**pouvais**
tu	**peux**	tu	**pouvais**
il	**peut**	il	**pouvait**
nous	**pouvons**	nous	**pouvions**
vous	**pouvez**	vous	**pouviez**
ils	**peuvent**	ils	**pouvaient**

		FUTURE	
		je	**pourrai**
		tu	**pourras**
		il	**pourra**
		nous	**pourrons**
		vous	**pourrez**
		ils	**pourront**

IMPERATIVE		CONDITIONAL	
	not used	je	**pourrais**
		tu	**pourrais**
		il	**pourrait**
		nous	**pourrions**
		vous	**pourriez**
		ils	**pourraient**

PAST HISTORIC		PRESENT SUBJUNCTIVE	
je	pus	je	puisse
tu	pus	tu	puisses
il	put	il	puisse
nous	pûmes	nous	puissions
vous	pûtes	vous	puissiez
ils	purent	ils	puissent
PERFECT		PAST SUBJUNCTIVE	
j'	ai pu	je	pusse
tu	as pu	tu	pusses
il	a pu	il	pût
nous	avons pu	nous	pussions
vous	avez pu	vous	pussiez
ils	ont pu	ils	pussent

CONSTRUCTIONS
pouvoir faire to be able to do
il ne peut pas venir he can't come
il n'en peut plus he's tired out; he's had enough
il a été on ne peut plus aimable he couldn't have been
kinder

78 prendre
to take

also **entreprendre**
to undertake

PRESENT PARTICIPLE
prenant

se méprendre
to be mistaken

PAST PARTICIPLE
pris

surprendre
to surprise

PRESENT
je	prends
tu	prends
il	prend
nous	prenons
vous	prenez
ils	prennent

IMPERFECT
je	prenais
tu	prenais
il	prenait
nous	prenions
vous	preniez
ils	prenaient

FUTURE
je	prendrai
tu	prendras
il	prendra
nous	prendrons
vous	prendrez
ils	prendront

IMPERATIVE
prends
prenons
prenez

CONDITIONAL
je	prendrais
tu	prendrais
il	prendrait
nous	prendrions
vous	prendriez
ils	prendraient

PAST HISTORIC		PRESENT SUBJUNCTIVE	
je	pris	je	prenne
tu	pris	tu	prennes
il	prit	il	prenne
nous	prîmes	nous	prenions
vous	prîtes	vous	preniez
ils	prirent	ils	prennent

PERFECT		PAST SUBJUNCTIVE	
j'	ai pris	je	prisse
tu	as pris	tu	prisses
il	a pris	il	prît
nous	avons pris	nous	prissions
vous	avez pris	vous	prissiez
ils	ont pris	ils	prissent

CONSTRUCTIONS

prendre qch à qn   to take sth from sb
il l'a pris dans un tiroir/sur la table   he took it out of a drawer/from the table
prendre feu   to catch fire
prendre qn en amitié/en aversion   to take a liking/a dislike to sb

79 **promettre**
to promise

also **compromettre**
to compromise

PRESENT PARTICIPLE
promettant

PAST PARTICIPLE
promis

PRESENT		IMPERFECT	
je	**promets**	je	**promettais**
tu	**promets**	tu	**promettais**
il	**promet**	il	**promettait**
nous	**promettons**	nous	**promettions**
vous	**promettez**	vous	**promettiez**
ils	**promettent**	ils	**promettaient**

		FUTURE	
		je	**promettrai**
		tu	**promettras**
		il	**promettra**
		nous	**promettrons**
		vous	**promettrez**
		ils	**promettront**

IMPERATIVE		CONDITIONAL	
	promets	je	**promettrais**
	promettons	tu	**promettrais**
	promettez	il	**promettrait**
		nous	**promettrions**
		vous	**promettriez**
		ils	**promettraient**

PAST HISTORIC		PRESENT SUBJUNCTIVE	
je	promis	je	promette
tu	promis	tu	promettes
il	promit	il	promette
nous	promîmes	nous	promettions
vous	promîtes	vous	promettiez
ils	promirent	ils	promettent

PERFECT		PAST SUBJUNCTIVE	
j'	ai promis	je	promisse
tu	as promis	tu	promisses
il	a promis	il	promît
nous	avons promis	nous	promissions
vous	avez promis	vous	promissiez
ils	ont promis	ils	promissent

CONSTRUCTIONS

promettre qch à qn to promise sth to sb
promettre à qn de faire qch to promise sb to do sth
on nous promet du beau temps we're in for some fine
weather, they say
se promettre de faire to resolve to do

80 protéger
to protect

also **abréger**
to shorten

PRESENT PARTICIPLE
protégeant

alléger
to lighten

PAST PARTICIPLE
protégé

assiéger
to besiege

PRESENT
je	protège
tu	protèges
il	protège
nous	protégeons
vous	protégez
ils	protègent

IMPERFECT
je	protégeais
tu	protégeais
il	protégeait
nous	protégions
vous	protégiez
ils	protégeaient

FUTURE
je	protégerai
tu	protégeras
il	protégera
nous	protégerons
vous	protégerez
ils	protégeront

IMPERATIVE
protège
protégeons
protégez

CONDITIONAL
je	protégerais
tu	protégerais
il	protégerait
nous	protégerions
vous	protégeriez
ils	protégeraient

piéger
to booby-trap

PAST HISTORIC		PRESENT SUBJUNCTIVE	
je	protégeai	je	protège
tu	protégeas	tu	protèges
il	protégea	il	protège
nous	protégeâmes	nous	protégions
vous	protégeâtes	vous	protégiez
ils	protégèrent	ils	protègent
PERFECT		PAST SUBJUNCTIVE	
j'	ai protégé	je	protégeasse
tu	as protégé	tu	protégeasses
il	a protégé	il	protégeât
nous	avons protégé	nous	protégeassions
vous	avez protégé	vous	protégeassiez
ils	ont protégé	ils	protégeassent

CONSTRUCTIONS
se protéger de qch/contre qch   to protect oneself from
sth/against sth

81 recevoir
to receive

also **apercevoir**
to see

PRESENT PARTICIPLE
recevant

décevoir
to disappoint

PAST PARTICIPLE
reçu

percevoir
to perceive

PRESENT		IMPERFECT	
je	reçois	je	recevais
tu	reçois	tu	recevais
il	reçoit	il	recevait
nous	recevons	nous	recevions
vous	recevez	vous	receviez
ils	reçoivent	ils	recevaient

FUTURE	
je	recevrai
tu	recevras
il	recevra
nous	recevrons
vous	recevrez
ils	recevront

IMPERATIVE	CONDITIONAL	
reçois	je	recevrais
recevons	tu	recevrais
recevez	il	recevrait
	nous	recevrions
	vous	recevriez
	ils	recevraient

PAST HISTORIC		PRESENT SUBJUNCTIVE	
je	reçus	je	reçoive
tu	reçus	tu	reçoives
il	reçut	il	reçoive
nous	reçûmes	nous	recevions
vous	reçûtes	vous	receviez
ils	reçurent	ils	reçoivent

PERFECT		PAST SUBJUNCTIVE	
j'	ai reçu	je	reçusse
tu	as reçu	tu	reçusses
il	a reçu	il	reçût
nous	avons reçu	nous	reçussions
vous	avez reçu	vous	reçussiez
ils	ont reçu	ils	reçussent

CONSTRUCTIONS

recevoir un cadeau de qn   to receive a present from sb
être reçu à un examen   to pass an exam
être reçu à l'université   to get a place at university
il a reçu un coup de pied   he got kicked

82 rendre
to give back

PRESENT PARTICIPLE
rendant

PAST PARTICIPLE
rendu

PRESENT		IMPERFECT	
je	**rends**	je	**rendais**
tu	**rends**	tu	**rendais**
il	**rend**	il	**rendait**
nous	**rendons**	nous	**rendions**
vous	**rendez**	vous	**rendiez**
ils	**rendent**	ils	**rendaient**

FUTURE	
je	**rendrai**
tu	**rendras**
il	**rendra**
nous	**rendrons**
vous	**rendrez**
ils	**rendront**

IMPERATIVE	CONDITIONAL	
rends	je	**rendrais**
rendons	tu	**rendrais**
rendez	il	**rendrait**
	nous	**rendrions**
	vous	**rendriez**
	ils	**rendraient**

to give back

PAST HISTORIC		PRESENT SUBJUNCTIVE	
je	rendis	je	rende
tu	rendis	tu	rendes
il	rendit	il	rende
nous	rendîmes	nous	rendions
vous	rendîtes	vous	rendiez
ils	rendirent	ils	rendent

PERFECT		PAST SUBJUNCTIVE	
j'	ai rendu	je	rendisse
tu	as rendu	tu	rendisses
il	a rendu	il	rendît
nous	avons rendu	nous	rendissions
vous	avez rendu	vous	rendissiez
ils	ont rendu	ils	rendissent

CONSTRUCTIONS

rendre qch à qn to give sth back to sb
rendre qn heureux to make sb happy
rendre visite à qn to pay sb a visit
se rendre to surrender
se rendre compte de qch to realize sth

83 rentrer
to go back; to go in

PRESENT PARTICIPLE
rentrant

PAST PARTICIPLE
rentré

PRESENT		IMPERFECT	
je	**rentre**	je	**rentrais**
tu	**rentres**	tu	**rentrais**
il	**rentre**	il	**rentrait**
nous	**rentrons**	nous	**rentrions**
vous	**rentrez**	vous	**rentriez**
ils	**rentrent**	ils	**rentraient**

FUTURE	
je	**rentrerai**
tu	**rentreras**
il	**rentrera**
nous	**rentrerons**
vous	**rentrerez**
ils	**rentreront**

IMPERATIVE	CONDITIONAL	
rentre	je	**rentrerais**
rentrons	tu	**rentrerais**
rentrez	il	**rentrerait**
	nous	**rentrerions**
	vous	**rentreriez**
	ils	**rentreraient**

to go back; to go in

PAST HISTORIC		PRESENT SUBJUNCTIVE	
je	rentrai	je	rentre
tu	rentras	tu	rentres
il	rentra	il	rentre
nous	rentrâmes	nous	rentrions
vous	rentrâtes	vous	rentriez
ils	rentrèrent	ils	rentrent

PERFECT		PAST SUBJUNCTIVE	
je	suis rentré	je	rentrasse
tu	es rentré	tu	rentrasses
il	est rentré	il	rentrât
nous	sommes rentrés	nous	rentrassions
vous	êtes rentré(s)	vous	rentrassiez
ils	sont rentrés	ils	rentrassent

CONSTRUCTIONS

rentrer à la maison   to go back home
rentrer dans une firme   to join a firm
rentrer dans un arbre   to crash into a tree
il a rentré la voiture   he put the car away
rentrer ses griffes   to draw in one's claws

84 répondre
to answer

also **confondre**
to confuse

PRESENT PARTICIPLE
répondant

correspondre
to correspond

PAST PARTICIPLE
répondu

tondre
to shear

PRESENT		IMPERFECT	
je	réponds	je	répondais
tu	réponds	tu	répondais
il	répond	il	répondait
nous	répondons	nous	répondions
vous	répondez	vous	répondiez
ils	répondent	ils	répondaient

		FUTURE	
		je	répondrai
		tu	répondras
		il	répondra
		nous	répondrons
		vous	répondrez
		ils	répondront

IMPERATIVE	CONDITIONAL	
réponds	je	répondrais
répondons	tu	répondrais
répondez	il	répondrait
	nous	répondrions
	vous	répondriez
	ils	répondraient

to answer

PAST HISTORIC		PRESENT SUBJUNCTIVE	
je	répondis	je	réponde
tu	répondis	tu	répondes
il	répondit	il	réponde
nous	répondîmes	nous	répondions
vous	répondîtes	vous	répondiez
ils	répondirent	ils	répondent

PERFECT		PAST SUBJUNCTIVE	
j'	ai répondu	je	répondisse
tu	as répondu	tu	répondisses
il	a répondu	il	répondît
nous	avons répondu	nous	répondissions
vous	avez répondu	vous	répondissiez
ils	ont répondu	ils	répondissent

CONSTRUCTIONS

répondre à qn/à une question   to answer sb/a question
on a sonné – va répondre   that's the bell – go and answer the door
ça ne répond pas   there's no reply
répondre de qn   to answer for sb

85 résoudre
to solve

PRESENT PARTICIPLE
résolvant

PAST PARTICIPLE
résolu

PRESENT		IMPERFECT	
je	**résous**	je	**résolvais**
tu	**résous**	tu	**résolvais**
il	**résout**	il	**résolvait**
nous	**résolvons**	nous	**résolvions**
vous	**résolvez**	vous	**résolviez**
ils	**résolvent**	ils	**résolvaient**

		FUTURE	
		je	**résoudrai**
		tu	**résoudras**
		il	**résoudra**
		nous	**résoudrons**
		vous	**résoudrez**
		ils	**résoudront**

IMPERATIVE		CONDITIONAL	
	résous	je	**résoudrais**
	résolvons	tu	**résoudrais**
	résolvez	il	**résoudrait**
		nous	**résoudrions**
		vous	**résoudriez**
		ils	**résoudraient**

PAST HISTORIC		PRESENT SUBJUNCTIVE	
je	résolus	je	résolve
tu	résolus	tu	résolves
il	résolut	il	résolve
nous	résolûmes	nous	résolvions
vous	résolûtes	vous	résolviez
ils	résolurent	ils	résolvent

PERFECT		PAST SUBJUNCTIVE	
j'	ai résolu	je	résolusse
tu	as résolu	tu	résolusses
il	a résolu	il	résolût
nous	avons résolu	nous	résolussions
vous	avez résolu	vous	résolussiez
ils	ont résolu	ils	résolussent

CONSTRUCTIONS
se résoudre à faire qch to resolve to do sth
être résolu à faire to be set on doing

86 rester
to remain

PRESENT PARTICIPLE
restant

PAST PARTICIPLE
resté

PRESENT		IMPERFECT	
je	**reste**	je	**restais**
tu	**restes**	tu	**restais**
il	**reste**	il	**restait**
nous	**restons**	nous	**restions**
vous	**restez**	vous	**restiez**
ils	**restent**	ils	**restaient**
		FUTURE	
		je	**resterai**
		tu	**resteras**
		il	**restera**
		nous	**resterons**
		vous	**resterez**
		ils	**resteront**
IMPERATIVE		CONDITIONAL	
	reste	je	**resterais**
	restons	tu	**resterais**
	restez	il	**resterait**
		nous	**resterions**
		vous	**resteriez**
		ils	**resteraient**

PAST HISTORIC		PRESENT SUBJUNCTIVE	
je	restai	je	reste
tu	restas	tu	restes
il	resta	il	reste
nous	restâmes	nous	restions
vous	restâtes	vous	restiez
ils	restèrent	ils	restent

PERFECT		PAST SUBJUNCTIVE	
je	suis resté	je	restasse
tu	es resté	tu	restasses
il	est resté	il	restât
nous	sommes restés	nous	restassions
vous	êtes resté(s)	vous	restassiez
ils	sont restés	ils	restassent

CONSTRUCTIONS

il est resté à regarder la télévision   he stayed watching television

c'est tout l'argent qui leur reste   that's all the money they have left

il reste encore un peu de pain   there's still a little bread left

87 retourner
to return

PRESENT PARTICIPLE
retournant

PAST PARTICIPLE
retourné

PRESENT		IMPERFECT	
je	**retourne**	je	**retournais**
tu	**retournes**	tu	**retournais**
il	**retourne**	il	**retournait**
nous	**retournons**	nous	**retournions**
vous	**retournez**	vous	**retourniez**
ils	**retournent**	ils	**retournaient**

		FUTURE	
		je	**retournerai**
		tu	**retourneras**
		il	**retournera**
		nous	**retournerons**
		vous	**retournerez**
		ils	**retourneront**

IMPERATIVE		CONDITIONAL	
	retourne	je	**retournerais**
	retournons	tu	**retournerais**
	retournez	il	**retournerait**
		nous	**retournerions**
		vous	**retourneriez**
		ils	**retourneraient**

PAST HISTORIC		PRESENT SUBJUNCTIVE	
je	retournai	je	retourne
tu	retournas	tu	retournes
il	retourna	il	retourne
nous	retournâmes	nous	retournions
vous	retournâtes	vous	retourniez
ils	retournèrent	ils	retournent

PERFECT		PAST SUBJUNCTIVE	
je	suis retourné	je	retournasse
tu	es retourné	tu	retournasses
il	est retourné	il	retournât
nous	sommes retournés	nous	retournassions
vous	êtes retourné(s)	vous	retournassiez
ils	sont retournés	ils	retournassent

CONSTRUCTIONS
il a retourné le seau/sac   he turned the bucket upside down/the bag inside out
il a retourné les marchandises   he sent the goods back
retourner en Italie   to go back to Italy
se retourner   to turn over; to turn round

88 revenir
to come back

PRESENT PARTICIPLE
revenant

PAST PARTICIPLE
revenu

PRESENT		IMPERFECT	
je	**reviens**	je	**revenais**
tu	**reviens**	tu	**revenais**
il	**revient**	il	**revenait**
nous	**revenons**	nous	**revenions**
vous	**revenez**	vous	**reveniez**
ils	**reviennent**	ils	**revenaient**

		FUTURE	
		je	**reviendrai**
		tu	**reviendras**
		il	**reviendra**
		nous	**reviendrons**
		vous	**reviendrez**
		ils	**reviendront**

IMPERATIVE	CONDITIONAL	
reviens	je	**reviendrais**
revenons	tu	**reviendrais**
revenez	il	**reviendrait**
	nous	**reviendrions**
	vous	**reviendriez**
	ils	**reviendraient**

PAST HISTORIC		PRESENT SUBJUNCTIVE	
je	revins	je	revienne
tu	revins	tu	reviennes
il	revint	il	revienne
nous	revînmes	nous	revenions
vous	revîntes	vous	reveniez
ils	revinrent	ils	reviennent

PERFECT		PAST SUBJUNCTIVE	
je	suis revenu	je	revinsse
tu	es revenu	tu	revinsses
il	est revenu	il	revînt
nous	sommes revenus	nous	revinssions
vous	êtes revenu(s)	vous	revinssiez
ils	sont revenus	ils	revinssent

CONSTRUCTIONS
le repas revient à 30 F the meal comes to 30 F
il est revenu à Paris he came back to Paris
il est revenu de Paris he's back from Paris
revenir sur une promesse to go back on a promise
revenir sur ses pas to retrace one's steps

89 rire

to laugh

also **sourire**

to smile

PRESENT PARTICIPLE
riant

PAST PARTICIPLE
ri

PRESENT		IMPERFECT	
je	ris	je	riais
tu	ris	tu	riais
il	rit	il	riait
nous	rions	nous	riions
vous	riez	vous	riiez
ils	rient	ils	riaient

		FUTURE	
		je	rirai
		tu	riras
		il	rira
		nous	rirons
		vous	rirez
		ils	riront

IMPERATIVE		CONDITIONAL	
	ris	je	rirais
	rions	tu	rirais
	riez	il	rirait
		nous	ririons
		vous	ririez
		ils	riraient

PAST HISTORIC		PRESENT SUBJUNCTIVE	
je	ris	je	rie
tu	ris	tu	ries
il	rit	il	rie
nous	rîmes	nous	riions
vous	rîtes	vous	riiez
ils	rirent	ils	rient

PERFECT		PAST SUBJUNCTIVE	
j'	ai ri	je	risse
tu	as ri	tu	risses
il	a ri	il	rît
nous	avons ri	nous	rissions
vous	avez ri	vous	rissiez
ils	ont ri	ils	rissent

CONSTRUCTIONS

rire de qn/qch   to laugh at sb/sth
il a fait cela pour rire   he did it for a joke
rire aux éclats   to roar with laughter

90 rompre
to break

also **corrompre**
to corrupt

PRESENT PARTICIPLE
rompant

interrompre
to interrupt

PAST PARTICIPLE
rompu

PRESENT		IMPERFECT	
je	romps	je	rompais
tu	romps	tu	rompais
il	rompt	il	rompait
nous	rompons	nous	rompions
vous	rompez	vous	rompiez
ils	rompent	ils	rompaient

		FUTURE	
		je	romprai
		tu	rompras
		il	rompra
		nous	romprons
		vous	romprez
		ils	rompront

IMPERATIVE		CONDITIONAL	
	romps	je	romprais
	rompons	tu	romprais
	rompez	il	romprait
		nous	romprions
		vous	rompriez
		ils	rompraient

PAST HISTORIC		PRESENT SUBJUNCTIVE	
je	rompis	je	rompe
tu	rompis	tu	rompes
il	rompit	il	rompe
nous	rompîmes	nous	rompions
vous	rompîtes	vous	rompiez
ils	rompirent	ils	rompent

PERFECT		PAST SUBJUNCTIVE	
j'	ai rompu	je	rompisse
tu	as rompu	tu	rompisses
il	a rompu	il	rompît
nous	avons rompu	nous	rompissions
vous	avez rompu	vous	rompissiez
ils	ont rompu	ils	rompissent

CONSTRUCTIONS

ils ont rompu (leurs fiançailles) they've broken off their engagement
rompre les rangs to fall out
se rompre to break; to burst
être rompu (de fatigue) to be exhausted

91 savoir
to know

PRESENT PARTICIPLE
sachant

PAST PARTICIPLE
su

PRESENT		IMPERFECT	
je	sais	je	savais
tu	sais	tu	savais
il	sait	il	savait
nous	savons	nous	savions
vous	savez	vous	saviez
ils	savent	ils	savaient

		FUTURE	
		je	saurai
		tu	sauras
		il	saura
		nous	saurons
		vous	saurez
		ils	sauront

IMPERATIVE		CONDITIONAL	
	sache	je	saurais
	sachons	tu	saurais
	sachez	il	saurait
		nous	saurions
		vous	sauriez
		ils	sauraient

PAST HISTORIC		PRESENT SUBJUNCTIVE	
je	sus	je	sache
tu	sus	tu	saches
il	sut	il	sache
nous	sûmes	nous	sachions
vous	sûtes	vous	sachiez
ils	surent	ils	sachent

PERFECT		PAST SUBJUNCTIVE	
j'	ai su	je	susse
tu	as su	tu	susses
il	a su	il	sût
nous	avons su	nous	sussions
vous	avez su	vous	sussiez
ils	ont su	ils	sussent

CONSTRUCTIONS

savoir faire   to know how to do; to be able to do
je ne sais pas quoi faire   I don't know what to do
je vous ferai savoir   I'll let you know
à savoir   that is, namely
on ne sait jamais   you never can tell

92 sentir

to smell; to feel   *also* **consentir**
                to agree

PRESENT PARTICIPLE
sentant   **démentir**
                to deny

PAST PARTICIPLE
senti   **mentir**
                to lie

PRESENT		IMPERFECT	
je	sens	je	sentais
tu	sens	tu	sentais
il	sent	il	sentait
nous	sentons	nous	sentions
vous	sentez	vous	sentiez
ils	sentent	ils	sentaient

FUTURE	
je	sentirai
tu	sentiras
il	sentira
nous	sentirons
vous	sentirez
ils	sentiront

IMPERATIVE	CONDITIONAL	
sens	je	sentirais
sentons	tu	sentirais
sentez	il	sentirait
	nous	sentirions
	vous	sentiriez
	ils	sentiraient

ressentir
to feel

PAST HISTORIC		PRESENT SUBJUNCTIVE	
je	sentis	je	sente
tu	sentis	tu	sentes
il	sentit	il	sente
nous	sentîmes	nous	sentions
vous	sentîtes	vous	sentiez
ils	sentirent	ils	sentent

PERFECT		PAST SUBJUNCTIVE	
j'	ai senti	je	sentisse
tu	as senti	tu	sentisses
il	a senti	il	sentît
nous	avons senti	nous	sentissions
vous	avez senti	vous	sentissiez
ils	ont senti	ils	sentissent

CONSTRUCTIONS
sentir bon/mauvais to smell good *or* nice/bad
j'ai senti s'arrêter la voiture I felt the car stopping
se sentir mal/mieux to feel ill/better

93 servir
to serve

PRESENT PARTICIPLE
servant

PAST PARTICIPLE
servi

PRESENT		IMPERFECT	
je	**sers**	je	**servais**
tu	**sers**	tu	**servais**
il	**sert**	il	**servait**
nous	**servons**	nous	**servions**
vous	**servez**	vous	**serviez**
ils	**servent**	ils	**servaient**

		FUTURE	
		je	**servirai**
		tu	**serviras**
		il	**servira**
		nous	**servirons**
		vous	**servirez**
		ils	**serviront**

IMPERATIVE		CONDITIONAL	
	sers	je	**servirais**
	servons	tu	**servirais**
	servez	il	**servirait**
		nous	**servirions**
		vous	**serviriez**
		ils	**serviraient**

PAST HISTORIC		PRESENT SUBJUNCTIVE	
je	servis	je	serve
tu	servis	tu	serves
il	servit	il	serve
nous	servîmes	nous	servions
vous	servîtes	vous	serviez
ils	servirent	ils	servent

PERFECT		PAST SUBJUNCTIVE	
j'	ai servi	je	servisse
tu	as servi	tu	servisses
il	a servi	il	servît
nous	avons servi	nous	servissions
vous	avez servi	vous	servissiez
ils	ont servi	ils	servissent

CONSTRUCTIONS

servir un plat à qn   to serve sb with a dish
servir à qn/à qch   to be useful to sb/for sth
servir à faire   to be used for doing
à quoi sert de pleurer?   what's the use of crying?
servir de   to act as; to serve as
se servir d'un plat   to help oneself to a dish

94 songer
to think

also **plonger**
to dive

PRESENT PARTICIPLE
songeant

prolonger
to prolong

PAST PARTICIPLE
songé

rallonger
to lengthen

PRESENT		IMPERFECT	
je	songe	je	songeais
tu	songes	tu	songeais
il	songe	il	songeait
nous	songeons	nous	songions
vous	songez	vous	songiez
ils	songent	ils	songeaient

		FUTURE	
		je	songerai
		tu	songeras
		il	songera
		nous	songerons
		vous	songerez
		ils	songeront

IMPERATIVE		CONDITIONAL	
	songe	je	songerais
	songeons	tu	songerais
	songez	il	songerait
		nous	songerions
		vous	songeriez
		ils	songeraient

ronger
to gnaw

PAST HISTORIC		PRESENT SUBJUNCTIVE	
je	songeai	je	songe
tu	songeas	tu	songes
il	songea	il	songe
nous	songeâmes	nous	songions
vous	songeâtes	vous	songiez
ils	songèrent	ils	songent

PERFECT		PAST SUBJUNCTIVE	
j'	ai songé	je	songeasse
tu	as songé	tu	songeasses
il	a songé	il	songeât
nous	avons songé	nous	songeassions
vous	avez songé	vous	songeassiez
ils	ont songé	ils	songeassent

CONSTRUCTIONS
songer à qch   to think sth over; to think of sth
songer à faire qch   to contemplate doing sth

95 sortir
to go out

also **ressortir**
to stand out

PRESENT PARTICIPLE
sortant

PAST PARTICIPLE
sorti

PRESENT		IMPERFECT	
je	sors	je	sortais
tu	sors	tu	sortais
il	sort	il	sortait
nous	sortons	nous	sortions
vous	sortez	vous	sortiez
ils	sortent	ils	sortaient

		FUTURE	
		je	sortirai
		tu	sortiras
		il	sortira
		nous	sortirons
		vous	sortirez
		ils	sortiront

IMPERATIVE		CONDITIONAL	
	sors	je	sortirais
	sortons	tu	sortirais
	sortez	il	sortirait
		nous	sortirions
		vous	sortiriez
		ils	sortiraient

PAST HISTORIC		PRESENT SUBJUNCTIVE	
je	sortis	je	sorte
tu	sortis	tu	sortes
il	sortit	il	sorte
nous	sortîmes	nous	sortions
vous	sortîtes	vous	sortiez
ils	sortirent	ils	sortent

PERFECT		PAST SUBJUNCTIVE	
je	suis sorti	je	sortisse
tu	es sorti	tu	sortisses
il	est sorti	il	sortît
nous	sommes sortis	nous	sortissions
vous	êtes sorti(s)	vous	sortissiez
ils	sont sortis	ils	sortissent

CONSTRUCTIONS

sortir d'une pièce/d'un pays to go (*or* come) out of a
room/leave a country

il a sorti la voiture du garage he got the car out of the
garage

sortir le chien to take the dog out

96 se souvenir
to remember

PRESENT PARTICIPLE
se souvenant

PAST PARTICIPLE
souvenu

PRESENT		IMPERFECT	
je	me souviens	je	me souvenais
tu	te souviens	tu	te souvenais
il	se souvient	il	se souvenait
nous	nous souvenons	nous	nous souvenions
vous	vous souvenez	vous	vous souveniez
ils	se souviennent	ils	se souvenaient

FUTURE	
je	me souviendrai
tu	te souviendras
il	se souviendra
nous	nous souviendrons
vous	vous souviendrez
ils	se souviendront

IMPERATIVE
souviens-toi
souvenons-nous
souvenez-vous

CONDITIONAL	
je	me souviendrais
tu	te souviendrais
il	se souviendrait
nous	nous souviendrions
vous	vous souviendriez
ils	se souviendraient

PAST HISTORIC		PRESENT SUBJUNCTIVE	
je	me souvins	je	me souvienne
tu	te souvins	tu	te souviennes
il	se souvint	il	se souvienne
nous	nous souvînmes	nous	nous souvenions
vous	vous souvîntes	vous	vous souveniez
ils	se souvinrent	ils	se souviennent

PERFECT		PAST SUBJUNCTIVE	
je	me suis souvenu	je	me souvinsse
tu	t'es souvenu	tu	te souvinsses
il	s'est souvenu	il	se souvînt
nous	nous sommes souvenus	nous	nous souvinssions
vous	vous êtes souvenu(s)	vous	vous souvinssiez
ils	se sont souvenus	ils	se souvinssent

CONSTRUCTIONS
se souvenir de qn/qch to remember sb/sth
se souvenir d'avoir fait qch to remember doing sth

97 suffire
to be enough

PRESENT PARTICIPLE
suffisant

PAST PARTICIPLE
suffi

PRESENT		IMPERFECT	
je	suffis	je	suffisais
tu	suffis	tu	suffisais
il	suffit	il	suffisait
nous	suffisons	nous	suffisions
vous	suffisez	vous	suffisiez
ils	suffisent	ils	suffisaient

		FUTURE	
		je	suffirai
		tu	suffiras
		il	suffira
		nous	suffirons
		vous	suffirez
		ils	suffiront

IMPERATIVE		CONDITIONAL	
	suffis	je	suffirais
	suffisons	tu	suffirais
	suffisez	il	suffirait
		nous	suffirions
		vous	suffiriez
		ils	suffiraient

PAST HISTORIC		PRESENT SUBJUNCTIVE	
je	suffis	je	suffise
tu	suffis	tu	suffises
il	suffit	il	suffise
nous	suffîmes	nous	suffisions
vous	suffîtes	vous	suffisiez
ils	suffirent	ils	suffisent

PERFECT		PAST SUBJUNCTIVE	
j'	ai suffi	je	suffisse
tu	as suffi	tu	suffisses
il	a suffi	il	suffît
nous	avons suffi	nous	suffissions
vous	avez suffi	vous	suffissiez
ils	ont suffi	ils	suffissent

CONSTRUCTIONS

suffire à or **pour faire**   to be sufficient or enough to do
suffire à qn   to be enough for sb
(ça) suffit!   that's enough!, that will do!
il suffit de 2 heures pour y aller   2 hours is enough to get there

98 suivre
to follow

also **poursuivre**
to pursue

PRESENT PARTICIPLE
suivant

PAST PARTICIPLE
suivi

PRESENT		IMPERFECT	
je	suis	je	suivais
tu	suis	tu	suivais
il	suit	il	suivait
nous	suivons	nous	suivions
vous	suivez	vous	suiviez
ils	suivent	ils	suivaient

		FUTURE	
		je	suivrai
		tu	suivras
		il	suivra
		nous	suivrons
		vous	suivrez
		ils	suivront

IMPERATIVE	CONDITIONAL	
suis	je	suivrais
suivons	tu	suivrais
suivez	il	suivrait
	nous	suivrions
	vous	suivriez
	ils	suivraient

PAST HISTORIC		PRESENT SUBJUNCTIVE	
je	suivis	je	suive
tu	suivis	tu	suives
il	suivit	il	suive
nous	suivîmes	nous	suivions
vous	suivîtes	vous	suiviez
ils	suivirent	ils	suivent

PERFECT		PAST SUBJUNCTIVE	
j'	ai suivi	je	suivisse
tu	as suivi	tu	suivisses
il	a suivi	il	suivît
nous	avons suivi	nous	suivissions
vous	avez suivi	vous	suivissiez
ils	ont suivi	ils	suivissent

CONSTRUCTIONS

suivre un régime   to be on a diet
suivre une classe   to attend a class
faire suivre son courrier   to have one's mail forwarded

99 surseoir
to defer

PRESENT PARTICIPLE
sursoyant

PAST PARTICIPLE
sursis

PRESENT		IMPERFECT	
je	**sursois**	je	**sursoyais**
tu	**sursois**	tu	**sursoyais**
il	**sursoit**	il	**sursoyait**
nous	**sursoyons**	nous	**sursoyions**
vous	**sursoyez**	vous	**sursoyiez**
ils	**sursoient**	ils	**sursoyaient**

		FUTURE	
		je	**surseoirai**
		tu	**surseoiras**
		il	**surseoira**
		nous	**surseoirons**
		vous	**surseoirez**
		ils	**surseoiront**

IMPERATIVE	CONDITIONAL	
sursois	je	**surseoirais**
sursoyons	tu	**surseoirais**
sursoyez	il	**surseoirait**
	nous	**surseoirions**
	vous	**surseoiriez**
	ils	**surseoiraient**

PAST HISTORIC		PRESENT SUBJUNCTIVE	
je	sursis	je	sursoie
tu	sursis	tu	sursoies
il	sursit	il	sursoie
nous	sursîmes	nous	sursoyions
vous	sursîtes	vous	sursoyiez
ils	sursirent	ils	sursoient

PERFECT		PAST SUBJUNCTIVE	
j'	ai sursis	je	sursisse
tu	as sursis	tu	sursisses
il	a sursis	il	sursît
nous	avons sursis	nous	sursissions
vous	avez sursis	vous	sursissiez
ils	ont sursis	ils	sursissent

CONSTRUCTIONS

surseoir à qch to defer *or* postpone sth

100 se taire
to stop talking

PRESENT PARTICIPLE
se taisant

PAST PARTICIPLE
tu

PRESENT		IMPERFECT	
je	me tais	je	me taisais
tu	te tais	tu	te taisais
il	se tait	il	se taisait
nous	nous taisons	nous	nous taisions
vous	vous taisez	vous	vous taisiez
ils	se taisent	ils	se taisaient

		FUTURE	
		je	me tairai
		tu	te tairas
		il	se taira
		nous	nous tairons
		vous	vous tairez
		ils	se tairont

IMPERATIVE	CONDITIONAL	
tais-toi	je	me tairais
taisons-nous	tu	te tairais
taisez-vous	il	se tairait
	nous	nous tairions
	vous	vous tairiez
	ils	se tairaient

PAST HISTORIC		PRESENT SUBJUNCTIVE	
je	me tus	je	me taise
tu	te tus	tu	te taises
il	se tut	il	se taise
nous	nous tûmes	nous	nous taisions
vous	vous tûtes	vous	vous taisiez
ils	se turent	ils	se taisent

PERFECT		PAST SUBJUNCTIVE	
je	me suis tu	je	me tusse
tu	t'es tu	tu	te tusses
il	s'est tu	il	se tût
nous	nous sommes tus	nous	nous tussions
vous	vous êtes tu(s)	vous	vous tussiez
ils	se sont tus	ils	se tussent

CONSTRUCTIONS

ils se sont tus   they stopped talking
taisez-vous!   be quiet!
se taire sur qch   to keep quiet about sth

101 tenir
to hold

also **appartenir**
to belong

PRESENT PARTICIPLE
tenant

contenir
to contain

PAST PARTICIPLE
tenu

entretenir
to maintain

PRESENT		IMPERFECT	
je	tiens	je	tenais
tu	tiens	tu	tenais
il	tient	il	tenait
nous	tenons	nous	tenions
vous	tenez	vous	teniez
ils	tiennent	ils	tenaient

		FUTURE	
		je	tiendrai
		tu	tiendras
		il	tiendra
		nous	tiendrons
		vous	tiendrez
		ils	tiendront

IMPERATIVE		CONDITIONAL	
tiens		je	tiendrais
tenons		tu	tiendrais
tenez		il	tiendrait
		nous	tiendrions
		vous	tiendriez
		ils	tiendraient

soutenir
to support

PAST HISTORIC		PRESENT SUBJUNCTIVE	
je	tins	je	tienne
tu	tins	tu	tiennes
il	tint	il	tienne
nous	tînmes	nous	tenions
vous	tîntes	vous	teniez
ils	tinrent	ils	tiennent

PERFECT		PAST SUBJUNCTIVE	
j'	ai tenu	je	tinsse
tu	as tenu	tu	tinsses
il	a tenu	il	tînt
nous	avons tenu	nous	tinssions
vous	avez tenu	vous	tinssiez
ils	ont tenu	ils	tinssent

CONSTRUCTIONS
tenir à to be attached to; to care about
tenir à faire to be keen to do
il ne tient qu'à vous de décider it's up to you to decide
se tenir to stand; to take place
être tenu de faire to be obliged to do

102 tomber
to fall

also **retomber**
to fall back

PRESENT PARTICIPLE
tombant

PAST PARTICIPLE
tombé

PRESENT		IMPERFECT	
je	tombe	je	tombais
tu	tombes	tu	tombais
il	tombe	il	tombait
nous	tombons	nous	tombions
vous	tombez	vous	tombiez
ils	tombent	ils	tombaient

		FUTURE	
		je	tomberai
		tu	tomberas
		il	tombera
		nous	tomberons
		vous	tomberez
		ils	tomberont

IMPERATIVE		CONDITIONAL	
	tombe	je	tomberais
	tombons	tu	tomberais
	tombez	il	tomberait
		nous	tomberions
		vous	tomberiez
		ils	tomberaient

to fall

PAST HISTORIC		PRESENT SUBJUNCTIVE	
je	tombai	je	tombe
tu	tombas	tu	tombes
il	tomba	il	tombe
nous	tombâmes	nous	tombions
vous	tombâtes	vous	tombiez
ils	tombèrent	ils	tombent

PERFECT		PAST SUBJUNCTIVE	
je	suis tombé	je	tombasse
tu	es tombé	tu	tombasses
il	est tombé	il	tombât
nous	sommes tombés	nous	tombassions
vous	êtes tombé(s)	vous	tombassiez
ils	sont tombés	ils	tombassent

CONSTRUCTIONS

tomber de bicyclette/cheval   to fall off one's
bicycle/horse
laisser tomber qch   to drop sth
faire tomber   to knock over; to knock down
tomber malade/amoureux   to fall ill/in love
tomber sur   to come across

103 traduire
to translate

PRESENT PARTICIPLE
traduisant

PAST PARTICIPLE
traduit

PRESENT		IMPERFECT	
je	traduis	je	traduisais
tu	traduis	tu	traduisais
il	traduit	il	traduisait
nous	traduisons	nous	traduisions
vous	traduisez	vous	traduisiez
ils	traduisent	ils	traduisaient

		FUTURE	
		je	traduirai
		tu	traduiras
		il	traduira
		nous	traduirons
		vous	traduirez
		ils	traduiront

IMPERATIVE	CONDITIONAL	
traduis	je	traduirais
traduisons	tu	traduirais
traduisez	il	traduirait
	nous	traduirions
	vous	traduiriez
	ils	traduiraient

PAST HISTORIC		PRESENT SUBJUNCTIVE	
je	traduisis	je	traduise
tu	traduisis	tu	traduises
il	traduisit	il	traduise
nous	traduisîmes	nous	traduisions
vous	traduisîtes	vous	traduisiez
ils	traduisirent	ils	traduisent

PERFECT		PAST SUBJUNCTIVE	
j'	ai traduit	je	traduisisse
tu	as traduit	tu	traduisisses
il	a traduit	il	traduisît
nous	avons traduit	nous	traduisissions
vous	avez traduit	vous	traduisissiez
ils	ont traduit	ils	traduisissent

CONSTRUCTIONS
traduit en/du français   translated into/from French

104 traire
to milk

also **distraire**
to distract

PRESENT PARTICIPLE
trayant

extraire
to extract

PAST PARTICIPLE
trait

soustraire
to subtract

PRESENT		IMPERFECT	
je	trais	je	trayais
tu	trais	tu	trayais
il	trait	il	trayait
nous	trayons	nous	trayions
vous	trayez	vous	trayiez
ils	traient	ils	trayaient

		FUTURE	
		je	trairai
		tu	trairas
		il	traira
		nous	trairons
		vous	trairez
		ils	trairont

IMPERATIVE		CONDITIONAL	
	trais	je	trairais
	trayons	tu	trairais
	trayez	il	trairait
		nous	trairions
		vous	trairiez
		ils	trairaient

to milk

PAST HISTORIC	PRESENT SUBJUNCTIVE	
not used	je	traie
	tu	traies
	il	traie
	nous	trayions
	vous	trayiez
	ils	traient

PERFECT		PAST SUBJUNCTIVE
j'	ai trait	*not used*
tu	as trait	
il	a trait	
nous	avons trait	
vous	avez trait	
ils	ont trait	

105 vaincre
to defeat

also **convaincre**
to convince

PRESENT PARTICIPLE
vainquant

PAST PARTICIPLE
vaincu

PRESENT
je	vaincs
tu	vaincs
il	vainc
nous	vainquons
vous	vainquez
ils	vainquent

IMPERFECT
je	vainquais
tu	vainquais
il	vainquait
nous	vainquions
vous	vainquiez
ils	vainquaient

FUTURE
je	vaincrai
tu	vaincras
il	vaincra
nous	vaincrons
vous	vaincrez
ils	vaincront

IMPERATIVE
vaincs
vainquons
vainquez

CONDITIONAL
je	vaincrais
tu	vaincrais
il	vaincrait
nous	vaincrions
vous	vaincriez
ils	vaincraient

PAST HISTORIC		PRESENT SUBJUNCTIVE	
je	vainquis	je	vainque
tu	vainquis	tu	vainques
il	vainquit	il	vainque
nous	vainquîmes	nous	vainquions
vous	vainquîtes	vous	vainquiez
ils	vainquirent	ils	vainquent

PERFECT		PAST SUBJUNCTIVE	
j'	ai vaincu	je	vainquisse
tu	as vaincu	tu	vainquisses
il	a vaincu	il	vainquît
nous	avons vaincu	nous	vainquissions
vous	avez vaincu	vous	vainquissiez
ils	ont vaincu	ils	vainquissent

CONSTRUCTIONS

s'avouer vaincu   to admit defeat

106 valoir
to be worth

PRESENT PARTICIPLE
valant

PAST PARTICIPLE
valu

PRESENT		IMPERFECT	
je	**vaux**	je	**valais**
tu	**vaux**	tu	**valais**
il	**vaut**	il	**valait**
nous	**valons**	nous	**valions**
vous	**valez**	vous	**valiez**
ils	**valent**	ils	**valaient**

		FUTURE	
		je	**vaudrai**
		tu	**vaudras**
		il	**vaudra**
		nous	**vaudrons**
		vous	**vaudrez**
		ils	**vaudront**

IMPERATIVE	CONDITIONAL	
vaux	je	**vaudrais**
valons	tu	**vaudrais**
valez	il	**vaudrait**
	nous	**vaudrions**
	vous	**vaudriez**
	ils	**vaudraient**

PAST HISTORIC		PRESENT SUBJUNCTIVE	
je	valus	je	vaille
tu	valus	tu	vailles
il	valut	il	vaille
nous	valûmes	nous	valions
vous	valûtes	vous	valiez
ils	valurent	ils	vaillent

PERFECT		PAST SUBJUNCTIVE	
j'	ai valu	je	valusse
tu	as valu	tu	valusses
il	a valu	il	valût
nous	avons valu	nous	valussions
vous	avez valu	vous	valussiez
ils	ont valu	ils	valussent

CONSTRUCTIONS
valoir cher/10 F   to be worth a lot/10 F
cet outil ne vaut rien   this tool is useless
il vaut mieux se taire   it's better to say nothing
ce film vaut la peine d'être vu   this film is worth seeing

107 vendre
to sell

also **défendre**
to defend

PRESENT PARTICIPLE
vendant

dépendre
to depend

PAST PARTICIPLE
vendu

entendre
to hear

PRESENT		IMPERFECT	
je	vends	je	vendais
tu	vends	tu	vendais
il	vend	il	vendait
nous	vendons	nous	vendions
vous	vendez	vous	vendiez
ils	vendent	ils	vendaient

		FUTURE	
		je	vendrai
		tu	vendras
		il	vendra
		nous	vendrons
		vous	vendrez
		ils	vendront

IMPERATIVE		CONDITIONAL	
	vends	je	vendrais
	vendons	tu	vendrais
	vendez	il	vendrait
		nous	vendrions
		vous	vendriez
		ils	vendraient

226

pendre
to hang

répandre
to spread

tendre
to stretch

PAST HISTORIC		PRESENT SUBJUNCTIVE	
je	vendis	je	vende
tu	vendis	tu	vendes
il	vendit	il	vende
nous	vendîmes	nous	vendions
vous	vendîtes	vous	vendiez
ils	vendirent	ils	vendent

PERFECT		PAST SUBJUNCTIVE	
j'	ai vendu	je	vendisse
tu	as vendu	tu	vendisses
il	a vendu	il	vendît
nous	avons vendu	nous	vendissions
vous	avez vendu	vous	vendissiez
ils	ont vendu	ils	vendissent

CONSTRUCTIONS
vendre qch à qn   to sell sb sth
il me l'a vendu 10 F   he sold it to me for 10 F
'à vendre'   'for sale'
ils se vendent à la pièce/douzaine   they are sold singly/by
the dozen

227

108 venir
to come

also **intervenir**
to intervene

PRESENT PARTICIPLE
venant

parvenir
to succeed

PAST PARTICIPLE
venu

survenir
to occur

PRESENT		IMPERFECT	
je	viens	je	venais
tu	viens	tu	venais
il	vient	il	venait
nous	venons	nous	venions
vous	venez	vous	veniez
ils	viennent	ils	venaient

		FUTURE	
		je	viendrai
		tu	viendras
		il	viendra
		nous	viendrons
		vous	viendrez
		ils	viendront

IMPERATIVE		CONDITIONAL	
	viens	je	viendrais
	venons	tu	viendrais
	venez	il	viendrait
		nous	viendrions
		vous	viendriez
		ils	viendraient

PAST HISTORIC		PRESENT SUBJUNCTIVE	
je	vins	je	vienne
tu	vins	tu	viennes
il	vint	il	vienne
nous	vînmes	nous	venions
vous	vîntes	vous	veniez
ils	vinrent	ils	viennent

PERFECT		PAST SUBJUNCTIVE	
je	suis venu	je	vinsse
tu	es venu	tu	vinsses
il	est venu	il	vînt
nous	sommes venus	nous	vinssions
vous	êtes venu(s)	vous	vinssiez
ils	sont venus	ils	vinssent

CONSTRUCTIONS

venir de Paris   to come from Paris
faire venir qn   to call *or* send for sb
venir de faire qch   to have just done sth
en venir à faire qch   to be reduced to doing sth

109 vêtir
to dress   *also* **revêtir**
                             to put on

PRESENT PARTICIPLE
vêtant

PAST PARTICIPLE
vêtu

PRESENT		IMPERFECT	
je	**vêts**	je	**vêtais**
tu	**vêts**	tu	**vêtais**
il	**vêt**	il	**vêtait**
nous	**vêtons**	nous	**vêtions**
vous	**vêtez**	vous	**vêtiez**
ils	**vêtent**	ils	**vêtaient**

FUTURE
je	**vêtirai**
tu	**vêtiras**
il	**vêtira**
nous	**vêtirons**
vous	**vêtirez**
ils	**vêtiront**

IMPERATIVE	CONDITIONAL	
vêts	je	**vêtirais**
vêtons	tu	**vêtirais**
vêtez	il	**vêtirait**
	nous	**vêtirions**
	vous	**vêtiriez**
	ils	**vêtiraient**

PAST HISTORIC		PRESENT SUBJUNCTIVE	
je	vêtis	je	vête
tu	vêtis	tu	vêtes
il	vêtit	il	vête
nous	vêtîmes	nous	vêtions
vous	vêtîtes	vous	vêtiez
ils	vêtirent	ils	vêtent

PERFECT		PAST SUBJUNCTIVE	
j'	ai vêtu	je	vêtisse
tu	as vêtu	tu	vêtisses
il	a vêtu	il	vêtît
nous	avons vêtu	nous	vêtissions
vous	avez vêtu	vous	vêtissiez
ils	ont vêtu	ils	vêtissent

CONSTRUCTIONS

vêtu d'un pantalon et d'un chandail   wearing trousers
and a sweater
se vêtir   to dress

231

110 vivre
to live

also **survivre**
to survive

PRESENT PARTICIPLE
vivant

PAST PARTICIPLE
vécu

PRESENT		IMPERFECT	
je	vis	je	vivais
tu	vis	tu	vivais
il	vit	il	vivait
nous	vivons	nous	vivions
vous	vivez	vous	viviez
ils	vivent	ils	vivaient

		FUTURE	
		je	vivrai
		tu	vivras
		il	vivra
		nous	vivrons
		vous	vivrez
		ils	vivront

IMPERATIVE		CONDITIONAL	
	vis	je	vivrais
	vivons	tu	vivrais
	vivez	il	vivrait
		nous	vivrions
		vous	vivriez
		ils	vivraient

PAST HISTORIC		PRESENT SUBJUNCTIVE	
je	vécus	je	vive
tu	vécus	tu	vives
il	vécut	il	vive
nous	vécûmes	nous	vivions
vous	vécûtes	vous	viviez
ils	vécurent	ils	vivent

PERFECT		PAST SUBJUNCTIVE	
j'	ai vécu	je	vécusse
tu	as vécu	tu	vécusses
il	a vécu	il	vécût
nous	avons vécu	nous	vécussions
vous	avez vécu	vous	vécussiez
ils	ont vécu	ils	vécussent

CONSTRUCTIONS

il vit à la campagne/en France   he lives in the country/in France

vivre de rentes/légumes   to live on a private income/on vegetables

il est facile/difficile à vivre   he's easy/difficult to get on with

233

111 voir
to see

also **entrevoir**
to catch a glimpse of

PRESENT PARTICIPLE
voyant

revoir
to revise

PAST PARTICIPLE
vu

PRESENT		IMPERFECT	
je	vois	je	voyais
tu	vois	tu	voyais
il	voit	il	voyait
nous	voyons	nous	voyions
vous	voyez	vous	voyiez
ils	voient	ils	voyaient

		FUTURE	
		je	verrai
		tu	verras
		il	verra
		nous	verrons
		vous	verrez
		ils	verront

IMPERATIVE		CONDITIONAL	
	vois	je	verrais
	voyons	tu	verrais
	voyez	il	verrait
		nous	verrions
		vous	verriez
		ils	verraient

PAST HISTORIC		PRESENT SUBJUNCTIVE	
je	vis	je	voie
tu	vis	tu	voies
il	vit	il	voie
nous	vîmes	nous	voyions
vous	vîtes	vous	voyiez
ils	virent	ils	voient

PERFECT		PAST SUBJUNCTIVE	
j'	ai vu	je	visse
tu	as vu	tu	visses
il	a vu	il	vît
nous	avons vu	nous	vissions
vous	avez vu	vous	vissiez
ils	ont vu	ils	vissent

CONSTRUCTIONS

aller voir qn   to go and see sb
faire voir qch   to show sth
on verra bien   we'll soon see
ça n'a rien à voir avec notre problème   it's got nothing to do with our problem
voyons!   come now!

112 vouloir
to want

PRESENT PARTICIPLE
voulant

PAST PARTICIPLE
voulu

PRESENT		IMPERFECT	
je	**veux**	je	**voulais**
tu	**veux**	tu	**voulais**
il	**veut**	il	**voulait**
nous	**voulons**	nous	**voulions**
vous	**voulez**	vous	**vouliez**
ils	**veulent**	ils	**voulaient**

		FUTURE	
		je	**voudrai**
		tu	**voudras**
		il	**voudra**
		nous	**voudrons**
		vous	**voudrez**
		ils	**voudront**

IMPERATIVE		CONDITIONAL	
	veuille	je	**voudrais**
	veuillons	tu	**voudrais**
	veuillez	il	**voudrait**
		nous	**voudrions**
		vous	**voudriez**
		ils	**voudraient**

to want

PAST HISTORIC		PRESENT SUBJUNCTIVE	
je	voulus	je	veuille
tu	voulus	tu	veuilles
il	voulut	il	veuille
nous	voulûmes	nous	voulions
vous	voulûtes	vous	vouliez
ils	voulurent	ils	veuillent

PERFECT		PAST SUBJUNCTIVE	
j'	ai voulu	je	voulusse
tu	as voulu	tu	voulusses
il	a voulu	il	voulût
nous	avons voulu	nous	voulussions
vous	avez voulu	vous	voulussiez
ils	ont voulu	ils	voulussent

CONSTRUCTIONS

vouloir faire qch to want to do sth
je veux bien le faire I'm happy to do it; I don't mind
doing it
en vouloir à qn to have something against sb
vouloir dire to mean

INDEX

(a) Each verb is numerically cross-referred to one of the 112 verb models shown in bold type. Defective verbs, however, are cross-referred to page 13.

(b) All entries are arranged in alphabetical order; for alphabetisation purposes, pronouns are not included: s'asseoir, se taire etc appear as asseoir (s'), taire (se) etc.

(c) With the exception of those verbs which are individually marked (see note (d)), and of Reflexive and Reciprocal verbs which are always conjugated with être, a verb's auxiliary is that of its verb model.

(d) Superior numbers refer you to notes on page 256, which outline how the verb deviates from its verb model.

(e) An asterisk (*) indicates that the verb is conjugated with être when intransitive and avoir when transitive.

239

chuchoter	36	complimenter	36	constater	36
circoncire[8]	97	compliquer	36	consterner	36
circonscrire	38	comporter	36	constituer	36
circonvenir[1]	108	composer	36	construire	29
circuler	36	composter	36	consulter	36
cirer	36	**comprendre**	**16**	contacter	36
ciseler	1	compromettre	79	contaminer	36
citer	36	compter	36	contempler	36
clarifier	25	concéder	41	contenir	101
classer	36	concentrer	36	contenter	36
classifier	25	concerner	36	conter	36
cligner	36	concevoir	81	contester	36
clignoter	36	concilier	25	continuer	36
clore	**14**	**conclure**	**17**	contraindre	23
clouer	36	concourir	21	contrarier	25
coder	36	concurrencer	15	contraster	36
codifier	25	condamner	36	contredire	48
cogner	36	condenser	36	contrefaire	43
coiffer	36	condescendre[1]	31	contrevenir[1]	108
coincer	15	**conduire**	**18**	contribuer	36
coïncider	36	conférer	41	contrôler	36
collaborer	36	confier	25	convaincre	105
collectionner	36	confire[9]	97	convenir[1]	108
coller	36	confirmer	36	convertir	45
coloniser	36	confisquer	36	convier	25
colorer	36	confondre	84	convoquer	36
colorier	25	conforter	36	coopérer	41
combattre	11	congédier	25	copier	25
combler	36	congeler	1	correspondre	84
commander	36	**connaître**	**19**	corriger	54
commémorer	36	conquérir	2	corrompre	90
commencer	**15**	consacrer	36	corroyer	63
commettre	56	conseiller	36	côtoyer	63
communier	25	consentir	92	coucher	36
communiquer	36	considérer	41	**coudre**	**20**
comparaître	67	consister	36	couler	36
comparer	36	consoler	36	couper	36
compenser	36	consolider	36	courber	36
complaire	74	consommer	36	**courir**	**21**
compléter	41	conspirer	36	coûter	36

dégriser	36	départager	54	désennuyer	63
déguerpir	45	départir (se)	68	désensibiliser	36
déguiser	36	dépasser	69	désentraver	36
déguster	36	dépayser	36	déséquilibrer	36
déjeter	50	dépecer	52	déserter	36
déjeuner	36	dépêcher	36	désespérer	41
déjouer	36	dépeindre	71	déshabiller	36
délaisser	36	dépendre	107	déshabituer	36
délayer	70	dépenser	36	déshériter	36
déléguer	41	dépérir	45	désigner	36
délibérer	41	dépister	36	désinfecter	36
délier	25	déplacer	15	désintégrer	41
délirer	36	déplaire	74	désintéresser	36
délivrer	36	déplier	25	désintoxiquer	36
déloger	54	déployer	63	désirer	36
demander	36	dépolir	45	désister (se)	36
démanteler	1	déposer	36	désobéir	45
démarquer	36	dépouiller	36	désoler	36
démarrer	36	dépoussiérer	41	désorganiser	36
démêler	36	déprécier	25	désorienter	36
déménager	54	déprendre	78	dessaisir	45
démener (se)	52	déprimer	36	dessécher	41
démentir	92	déraciner	36	desserrer	36
démettre	56	déranger	54	dessiner	36
demeurer[12]	36	déraper	36	destiner	36
démissionner	36	dérégler	41	destituer	36
démolir	45	déroger	54	désunir	45
démonter[1]	57	dérouler	36	détacher	36
démontrer	36	dérouter	36	détailler	36
démultiplier	25	désaccoutumer	36	détecter	36
démunir	45	désagréger	80	déteindre	71
dénaturer	36	désaltérer	41	dételer	4
dénier	25	désamorcer	15	détendre	107
dénigrer	36	désapprendre	5	détenir	101
déniveler	4	désapprouver	36	détériorer	36
dénombrer	36	désassortir	45	déterminer	36
dénoncer	15	désavantager	54	détester	36
dénouer	36	désavouer	36	détordre	58
dépanner	36	descendre*	31	détourner	36
dépaqueter	50	désemparer	36	détraquer	36

244

émouvoir[15]	61	enjoliver	36	épater	36
emparer (s')	36	enlacer	15	épeler	4
empêcher	36	enlever	52	éplucher	36
empiéter	41	enneiger	54	éponger	94
empirer	36	ennuyer	63	épouser	36
emplir	45	énoncer	15	épouvanter	36
employer	63	enquérir (s')	2	épreindre	71
empoisonner	36	enquêter	36	éprendre (s')	78
emporter	36	enraciner	36	éprouver	36
emprisonner	36	enrager	54	épuiser	36
emprunter	36	enregistrer	36	équilibrer	36
encadrer	36	enrichir	45	équiper	36
encaisser	36	enrouler	36	équivaloir	106
enchaîner	36	enseigner	36	esclaffer (s')	36
enchanter	36	ensevelir	45	escorter	36
encombrer	36	ensuivre (s')[3]	98	**espérer**	**41**
encourager	54	entamer	36	esquisser	36
encourir	21	entasser	36	esquiver	36
endetter	36	entendre	107	essayer	70
endoctriner	36	enterrer	36	essorer	36
endommager	54	enthousiasmer	36	essouffler	36
endormir (s')	37	entourer	36	essuyer	63
enduire	29	entraîner	36	estimer	36
endurcir	45	entraver	36	estropier	25
énerver	36	entrelacer	15	établir	45
enfanter	36	entremettre (s')	56	étaler	36
enfermer	36	entreprendre	78	étayer	70
enfiler	36	**entrer***	**39**	éteindre	71
enflammer	36	entretenir	101	étendre	107
enfler	36	entrevoir	111	éternuer	36
enfoncer	15	énumérer	41	étiqueter	50
enfouir	45	envahir	45	étirer	36
enfreindre	71	envelopper	36	étoffer	36
enfuir (s')	46	envisager	54	étonner	36
engager	54	envoler (s')	36	étouffer	36
engloutir	45	**envoyer**	**40**	étourdir	45
engourdir	45	épandre	107	étrangler	36
engraisser	36	épanouir	45	**être**	**42**
engueuler	36	épargner	36	étreindre	71
enivrer	36	éparpiller	36	étudier	25

246

froncer	15	gravir	45	heurter	36
frotter	36	greffer	36	hocher	36
frustrer	36	grêler	36	honorer	36
fuir	**46**	griffonner	36	horrifier	25
fumer	36	grignoter	36	huer	36
fusiller	36	griller	36	humaniser	36
gâcher	36	grimacer	15	humidifier	25
gagner	36	grimper	36	humilier	25
galoper	36	grincer	15	hurler	36
garantir	45	griser	36	hypnotiser	36
garder	36	grogner	36	idéaliser	36
garer	36	grommeler	4	identifier	25
garnir	45	gronder	36	ignorer	36
gaspiller	36	grossir	45	illuminer	36
gâter	36	grouiller	36	illustrer	36
gauchir	45	grouper	36	imaginer	36
gaufrer	36	guérir	45	imiter	36
gausser (se)	36	guerroyer	63	immigrer	36
geindre	71	guetter	36	immiscer (s')	15
geler	1	guider	36	immobiliser	36
gémir	45	guinder	36	immoler	36
gêner	36	habiller	36	impatienter	36
généraliser	36	habiter	36	impliquer	36
gérer	41	habituer	36	implorer	36
gésir	*page 13*	hacher	36	importer	36
giboyer	63	haïr	47	impressionner	36
gifler	36	haleter	1	imprimer	36
givrer	36	handicaper	36	improviser	36
glacer	15	hanter	36	inaugurer	36
glisser	36	harceler	4	inciter	36
glorifier	25	harmoniser	36	incliner	36
gommer	36	hasarder	36	inclure[18]	17
gonfler	36	hâter	36	incommoder	36
goûter	36	hausser	36	incorporer	36
gouverner	36	héberger	54	incriminer	36
gracier	25	hébéter	41	inculper	36
grandir	45	hennir	45	indiquer	36
gratifier	25	hérisser	36	induire	29
gratter	36	hériter	36	infecter	36
graver	36	hésiter	36	infester	36

infirmer	36	invoquer	36	lorgner	36
infliger	54	irriter	36	lotir	45
influencer	15	isoler	36	loucher	36
informer	36	jaillir	45	louer	36
ingénier (s')	25	jaser	36	louper	36
inhaler	36	jaunir	45	louvoyer	63
initier	25	**jeter**	**50**	lubrifier	25
injurier	25	jeûner	36	lutter	36
innover	36	**joindre**	**51**	mâcher	36
inoculer	36	jouer	36	machiner	36
inonder	36	jouir	45	magnifier	25
inquiéter	41	juger	54	maigrir	45
inscrire	38	jumeler	4	maintenir	101
insensibiliser	36	jurer	36	maîtriser	36
insérer	41	justifier	25	majorer	36
insinuer	36	labourer	36	malfaire	43
insister	36	lacer	15	malmener	52
inspecter	36	lâcher	36	maltraiter	36
inspirer	36	laisser	36	**manger**	**54**
installer	36	lamenter (se)	36	manier	25
instituer	36	lancer	15	manifester	36
instruire	29	languir	45	manigancer	15
insulter	36	larmoyer	63	manipuler	36
insurger (s')	54	laver	36	manœuvrer	36
intégrer	41	lécher	41	manquer	36
intensifier	25	légaliser	36	manufacturer	36
intercéder	41	légiférer	41	manutentionner	36
interdire	**48**	lésiner	36	marcher	36
intéresser	36	**lever**	**52**	marier	25
interloquer	36	libérer	41	marquer	36
interroger	54	licencier	25	marteler	1
interrompre	90	lier	25	masquer	36
intervenir	108	ligoter	36	massacrer	36
intituler	36	limer	36	masser	36
intriguer	36	limiter	36	matérialiser	36
introduire	**49**	liquéfier	25	**maudire**	**55**
inventer	36	liquider	36	maugréer	24
invertir	45	**lire**	**53**	mécaniser	36
investir	45	livrer	36	méconnaître	19
inviter	36	loger	54	mécontenter	36

médire	48	mortifier	25	obliger	54
méditer	36	motiver	36	oblitérer	41
méfaire	43	moucher	36	obscurcir	45
méfier (se)	25	**moudre**	**59**	obséder	41
mélanger	54	mouiller	36	observer	36
mêler	36	**mourir**	**60**	obstiner (s')	36
menacer	15	**mouvoir**	**61**	**obtenir**	**64**
ménager	54	muer	36	occuper	36
mendier	25	multiplier	25	octroyer	63
mener	52	munir	45	offenser	36
mentionner	36	mûrir	45	**offrir**	**65**
mentir	92	murmurer	36	oindre	*page 13*
méprendre (se)	78	museler	4	omettre	56
mépriser	36	muter	36	opérer	41
mériter	36	mutiler	36	opposer	36
messeoir	*page 13*	mystifier	25	opprimer	36
mesurer	36	nager	54	ordonner	36
mettre	**56**	**naître**	**62**	organiser	36
meubler	36	nantir	45	orner	36
meugler	36	narrer	36	orthographier	25
meurtrir	45	naviguer	36	osciller	36
miauler	36	navrer	36	oser	36
mijoter	36	nécessiter	36	ôter	36
mimer	36	négliger	54	oublier	25
miner	36	négocier	25	ouïr	*page 13*
minimiser	36	neiger	54	outrager	54
mobiliser	36	**nettoyer**	**63**	**ouvrir**	**66**
modeler	1	nier	25	oxyder	36
modérer	41	niveler	4	pacifier	25
moderniser	36	noircir	45	**paître**	*page 13*
modifier	25	nommer	36	pâlir	45
moisir	45	normaliser	36	palper	36
moissonner	36	noter	36	palpiter	36
mollir	45	nouer	36	panser	36
monnayer	70	nourrir	45	parachever	52
monopoliser	36	noyer	63	parachuter	36
monter★	**57**	nuire[19]	29	**paraître**	**67**
montrer	36	numéroter	36	paralyser	36
moquer (se)	36	obéir	45	parcourir	21
mordre	**58**	objecter	36	pardonner	36

parer	36	pétrifier	25	prédire	48
parfondre	84	pétrir	45	préférer	41
parfumer	36	peupler	36	préjuger	54
parier	25	photographier	25	prélever	52
parler	36	picoter	36	préméditer	36
parquer	36	piéger	80	**prendre**	**78**
partager	54	piétiner	36	préparer	36
participer	36	pincer	15	prescrire	38
partir	**68**	placer	15	présenter	36
parvenir	108	plaider	36	préserver	36
passer*	**69**	plaindre	23	présider	36
passionner	36	**plaire**	**74**	pressentir	92
patienter	36	plaisanter	36	présumer	36
pâtir	45	planifier	25	prétendre	107
pauser	36	plaquer	36	prêter	36
paver	36	pleurer	36	prévaloir[21]	106
pavoiser	36	**pleuvoir**	**75**	prévenir[1]	108
payer	**70**	plier	25	prévoir[22]	111
pêcher	36	plonger	94	prier	25
pécher	41	poindre	*page 13*	priver	36
peigner	36	polir	45	privilégier	25
peindre	**71**	polluer	36	procéder	41
peler	1	pomper	36	proclamer	36
pencher	36	ponctuer	36	procréer	24
pendre	107	pondre	84	produire	29
pénétrer	41	porter	36	profiter	36
penser	36	poser	36	progresser	36
percer	15	posséder	41	projeter	50
percevoir	81	poster	36	prolonger	94
perdre	**72**	poudroyer	63	promener	52
perfectionner	36	pourfendre	107	**promettre**	**79**
perforer	36	pourrir	45	promouvoir[23]	61
périr	45	poursuivre	98	prononcer	15
permettre	**73**	**pourvoir**	**76**	proposer	36
persécuter	36	pousser	36	proscrire	38
persévérer	41	**pouvoir[20]**	**77**	**protéger**	**80**
persister	36	pratiquer	36	protester	36
persuader	36	précéder	41	prouver	36
pervertir	45	prêcher	36	provenir	108
peser	52	préciser	36	publier	25

punir	45	rassembler	36	recueillir	28
purifier	25	rasséréner	41	recuire	29
qualifier	25	rassurer	36	reculer	36
quereller	36	rater	36	récupérer	41
questionner	36	rationaliser	36	recycler	36
quêter	36	rattraper	36	redescendre	31
quitter	36	ravir	45	rédiger	54
rabattre	11	ravitailler	36	redire	35
raccommoder	36	réagir	45	redoubler	36
raccompagner	36	réaliser	36	redouter	36
raccorder	36	rebattre	11	redresser	36
raccourcir	45	rebondir	45	réduire	29
raccrocher	36	rebuter	36	refaire	43
racheter	1	receler	1	référer	41
racler	36	recenser	36	refermer	36
racoler	36	recevoir	**81**	réfléchir	45
raconter	36	réchapper	36	refléter	41
raffermir	45	réchauffer	36	refondre	84
raffiner	36	rechercher	36	réformer	36
rafler	36	réciter	36	refroidir	45
rafraîchir	45	réclamer	36	réfugier (se)	25
ragaillardir	45	récolter	36	refuser	36
raidir	45	recommander	36	réfuter	36
railler	36	recommencer	15	regagner	36
raisonner	36	récompenser	36	regaillardir	45
rajeunir	45	réconcilier	25	regarder	36
rajouter	36	reconduire	18	régénérer	41
rajuster	36	réconforter	36	régir	45
ralentir	45	reconnaître	19	régler	41
rallier	25	reconquérir	2	régner	41
rallonger	94	reconstruire	29	regretter	36
rallumer	36	reconvertir	45	regrouper	36
ramasser	36	recopier	25	réhabiliter	36
ramener	52	recoudre	20	réhabituer	36
ramollir	45	recourir	21	rehausser	36
ranimer	36	recouvrir	22	réimprimer	36
rappeler	4	récréer	24	réintégrer	41
rapporter	36	récrier (se)	25	rejaillir	45
rapprocher	36	récrire	38	rejeter	50
raser	36	rectifier	25	rejoindre	51

tolérer	41	tricher	36	verdoyer	63
tomber	**102**	tricoter	36	vérifier	25
tondre	84	trier	25	vernir	45
tonner	36	triompher	36	verrouiller	36
tordre	58	tripoter	36	verser	36
torpiller	36	tromper	36	**vêtir**	**109**
tortiller	36	troquer	36	vexer	36
torturer	36	trotter	36	vibrer	36
toucher	36	troubler	36	vider	36
tourmenter	36	trouer	36	vieillir	45
tourner	36	trouver	36	violer	36
tournoyer	63	truffer	36	virer	36
tousser	36	truquer	36	viser	36
tracasser	36	tuer	36	visiter	36
tracer	15	tutoyer	63	visser	36
traduire	**103**	ulcérer	41	vitrifier	25
trahir	45	unifier	25	vitupérer	41
traîner	36	unir	45	vivifier	25
traire	**104**	urbaniser	36	**vivre**	**110**
traiter	36	user	36	vociférer	41
transcrire	38	usiner	36	voiler	36
transférer	41	utiliser	36	**voir**	**111**
transformer	36	vacciner	36	voler	36
transmettre	56	**vaincre**	**105**	vomir	45
transparaître	67	**valoir**	**106**	voter	36
transpirer	36	vanter	36	vouer	36
transplanter	36	varier	25	**vouloir**	**112**
transporter	36	végéter	41	vouvoyer	63
traquer	36	veiller	36	voyager	54
travailler	36	vendanger	54	vrombir	45
traverser	36	**vendre**	**107**	vulgariser	36
trébucher	36	venger	54	zébrer	41
trembler	36	**venir**	**108**	zézayer	70
tremper	36	verdir	45	zigzaguer	36

1) *Auxiliary* = avoir.
2) *Auxiliary* = être.
3) *Only infinitive and 3rd persons of each tense used.*
4) *Past participle:* absous, absoute; *Past Historic and Past Subjunctive not used.*
5) *Conjugated with either avoir or être.*
6) *No circumflex on:* j'accrois, tu accrois, j'accrus, tu accrus, il accrut, ils accrurent, j'accrusse *etc*, accru.
7) *Hardly used except in infinitive and 3rd persons of Present, Future and Conditional.*
8) *Past participle:* circoncis.
9) *Past participle:* confit.
10) *As for* (6).
11) *Present tense singular, Future and Conditional tenses least common.*
12) *'To live': auxiliary* = avoir; *'to remain': auxiliary* = être.
13) *Past participle:* dissous, dissoute; *Past Historic and Past Subjunctive not used.*
14) *Auxiliary* = être; *NB:* il éclot; *hardly used except in 3rd persons.*
15) *Past participle:* ému.
16) *'To prosper': present participle* = florissant; *Imperfect* = florissait.
17) *Past participle:* frit; *used mainly in singular of Present tense and in compound tenses.*
18) *Past participle:* inclus.
19) *Past participle:* nui.
20) *In interrogative form,* 'puis' *is substituted for* 'peux': puis-je vous aider? = *may I help you?*
21) *Present Subjunctive:* je prévale *etc.*
22) *Future:* je prévoirai *etc; Conditional:* je prévoirais *etc.*
23) *Past participle:* promu; *used only in infinitive, both participles, and compound tenses.*
24) *Past participle:* relui; *Past Historic:* je reluis *etc.*
25) *No past participle – no compound tenses.*